PEARLS
from the
PRACTICE of LIFE

D1176993

PEARLS

from the

PRACTICE of LIFE

A family physician's guide to help you struggle less and thrive more

JOHN CHUCK, M.D.

Published by Amazon KDP.

Interior layout and cover design: Carlene Vitale

ISBN 9798505312476

For my parents, James and Marie, who gave me life,
then modeled for me how to live it to the fullest.

TABLE OF CONTENTS

Introduction   1

PART I: FIRST THINGS FIRST

Chapter 1   Wired at Birth   11
Chapter 2   Choice Trumps Circumstances   15
Chapter 3   The Pursuit of Happiness   17
Chapter 4   Individual Achievement in a Team Environment   21
Chapter 5   Connection   23
Chapter 6   Listen More, Talk Less   25
Chapter 7   Friends for the Journey, Including Pallbearer Buddies   29
Chapter 8   A Strategy for Winning   33
Chapter 9   More "and," Less "but"   35
Chapter 10 Making Pretend Decisions   37
Chapter 11 Nobody's Looking at You   39

PART II: THE WORK WORLD

Chapter 12 Why You Need Money   43
Chapter 13 Why People Pay You   45
Chapter 14 Work Hard, Be Kind   47
Chapter 15 Show Up and Follow Through   49
Chapter 16 Be Flexible & Learn How to Get Along With
            Other People   53
Chapter 17 Creativity   55

Chapter 18   Calendars & Checklists   59
Chapter 19   Universally Wanted and Adored   61

PART III: LOFTY GOALS

Chapter 20   Going Public or Serving the Public?   65
Chapter 21   Breaking Away from the Thundering Herd   67
Chapter 22   Bending the Curve   71
Chapter 23   Paint the Picture-Perfect Postcard   73
Chapter 24   Values-Congruent Living   75
Chapter 25   Benevolence   77
Chapter 26   Mr. Williams' Wish   79
Chapter 27   We Need More Mingas   81
Chapter 28   Kiva Love   83
Chapter 29   The Moral Bucket List   85
Chapter 30   Authentic Humility   89
Chapter 31   Joy   91
Chapter 32   Leaving Your Mark   93
Chapter 33   Meaning   95
Chapter 34   The Trifecta   97
Chapter 35   "I'll Just Rent"   99
Chapter 36   Greatness Redefined   103

PART IV: GETTING THINGS DONE

Chapter 37   A Framework of Energy and Chapters   107
Chapter 38   Take Charge   109
Chapter 39   Lead from Where You Stand   111
Chapter 40   Use What You've Got   113
Chapter 41   Excellence   115
Chapter 42   Servant Leadership   117
Chapter 43   Appreciative Inquiry   121
Chapter 44   Diversity & Inclusion   125
Chapter 45   Inversion   127

Chapter 46   The Rider & The Elephant   131
Chapter 47   A Dynamic Duo   133
Chapter 48   The Intersection of D-I and PI   135
Chapter 49   The Elevator Pitch   139
Chapter 50   Non-Negotiables & Guardrails   141
Chapter 51   The Essential Role of Rest   143
Chapter 52   Live Outside the Box, and Get Sassy
             When Necessary   147
Chapter 53   Salmagundi   149

PART V: STRUGGLES

Chapter 54   Our Predicament   153
Chapter 55   Its Resolution   155
Chapter 56   Mindfulness   157
Chapter 57   Gratitude   159
Chapter 58   Cultivating Relationships   161
Chapter 59   Positive Adaptation   165
Chapter 60   Feed the Right Inner Wolf   169
Chapter 61   The Real Bad Asses   171
Chapter 62   Lessons from a Jet Fighter Pilot   177
Chapter 63   The Power of Story   179
Chapter 64   Foxhole Mantras   183

PART VI: DOCTOR STUFF

Chapter 65   Your Body & Brain Only Get Worse   191
Chapter 66   It's Mostly About Lifestyle Choices   205
Chapter 67   The King of All Health   211
Chapter 68   The Fifth Humor   219
Chapter 69   Enjoy Every Sandwich   223
             Thanks and Acknowledgments   225
             About the Author   231

INTRODUCTION

My Uncle Arthur was a solo practice general internist in Fresno. If you aren't familiar with Fresno, it's located in the heart of the fertile San Joaquin Valley, smack dab in the middle of California, halfway between Sacramento and Los Angeles. Think flat, hot, strip malls, raisins, and figs.

Uncle Art was a throwback doctor. Big smile. White short-sleeved shirt, silk tie, and black wingtip dress shoes. He carried a weathered black doctor's bag. Made house calls. Took care of people who could not afford to pay him because it was the right thing to do. Drove a silver Lincoln Continental with suicide doors and maneuvered its power-steering wheel with a single pinky finger.

Whenever he and Auntie Phyllis came to San Francisco for a weekend of fine dining and the performing arts, he would visit our family with his bag and take care of our various ills. My dad had high blood pressure. I always had a stomachache.

When Uncle Art died in the spring of 2010, we returned to Fresno for his memorial service. It was officiated by my father James, by then a retired minister who was enjoying a second chapter career as a professor at a seminary in Berkeley. The interment ceremony was held at Belmont Memorial Park, and our drive from the funeral home to Uncle Arthur's final resting place took us by Roeding Park, where as a young child I had enjoyed roller coaster and Ferris wheel rides during our annual summer visits with my maternal grandparents, Albert and Yuk-Wah Jing.

Uncle Arthur had lived a long and good life, so the ceremony was solemn but without the grief and despair associated with a life cut short or marred by tragedy. My father's comments were brief, but moving, and have remained with me to this day: "The saddest thing about life is not dying, for we all must die. The saddest thing about life is wasting the time you have."

This was a simple and powerful message from a man who had experienced a broad spectrum of the human condition through more than four decades of work as a pastor in San Francisco's Chinatown. It was a tenure that included shepherding his flock through countless births, marriages, victories, defeats, indignities, and deaths. Had I been an early adopter of Twitter, I would have posted my dad's comments followed by #TRUTH.

Thirty-two years earlier, in 1978, I was a high school senior and my professional dream was not to be a doctor or minister. I aspired to be a professional journalist for the Sporting Green of the *San Francisco Chronicle*, a separate section of the paper that was published on mint green newsprint.

I envisioned myself as a beat writer for the Giants, spending lazy days and frigid evenings at Candlestick Park, being a press box regular at Dodger Stadium and Wrigley Field, my body slowly growing a pot belly due to a sedentary lifestyle and steady diet of hot dogs on soft white buns.

However, one warm spring afternoon, while sitting in Flossie Lewis' Advanced Placement English class, I came to the sad realization that my chances of being paid to write were slim to none, given that I wasn't even the best writer in my cohort of thirty pimply teens. That title went to Cathy Winks, a brilliant and beautiful young woman who journeyed east to attend Barnard and later in life wrote a series of books about sex, including *Sexy Mamas: Keeping Your Sex Life Alive While Raising Kids* and *Good Vibrations Guide to Sex: The Most Complete Sex Manual Ever Written*.

The ministry was a poor fit for a lackadaisical Sunday school student like me who had no interest in memorizing scripture and whose limited vocal range made singing hymns an exercise in dancing between octaves. Given my interests in science and working with people, I decided to follow in Uncle Art's footsteps and pursue a career in medicine.

Pre-med days at Cal were followed by medical school at UCLA and a family practice residency at the UC Davis Medical Center in Sacramento. I joined The Permanente Medical Group (TPMG)—a large multi-specialty group practice—in 1989 and enjoyed a 31-year career of using everything I learned to help my patients fulfill their dreams and avoid premature disability and death. Midway through my career I became involved in helping physicians address the burnout that runs rampant in our profession and I finished my career as the regional chairperson of the physician health and wellness leaders group for my 10,000 colleagues.

In my roles as healer and physician wellness leader, I enjoyed a bird's-eye view of the many ways that my patients and colleagues dealt with our predicament as human beings, namely our suffering and mortality, lessons that I believe can serve as helpful blueprints for navigating life's struggles and finding joy and meaning.

At one point, the insights that I was collecting and passing on to my patients and colleagues became too numerous and unwieldy to remember and organize, so I started to record them on a private blog titled, "Pearls from the Practice of Life—family physician's compilation of short stories that highlight the human condition and the various and glorious ways that we contemplate and respond to our circumstances."

Why "pearls?" Lorin, Palazzi, and Turner define pearls as "small bits of free-standing, clinically relevant information based on experience or observation. They are part of the vast domain of experience-based medicine, and can be helpful for dealing with problems for which controlled data do not exist." Much as lustrous pearls are formed when mollusks respond to irritants by secreting layer upon layer of protective fluids that solidify to form dense jewels, physicians conquer disease by developing dense nuggets of life-saving knowledge and wisdom that they share with one another and pass on to the next generation of healers.

This book is a summary of what I believe are the most truthful and helpful pearls I have learned about life, and the stories about how I acquired them. Those that are rooted in traditional evidence-based science will appeal to your cerebral cortex and its higher order thinking and reasoning. Others are more intuitive and will resonate more with the limbic system that houses your emotions. Acknowledging and understanding both the cognitive and emotional drivers of human behavior will help you to better understand why you and others think, feel, and act the way you do. My hope is that you will enjoy these pearls and use them to waste less of the precious time that you have during your one brief life.

Older readers like myself who face a relatively short horizon have some natural motivation to do this work, to get things right before we die. Younger readers who are precocious or suffering might also feel motivated to learn and change. The rest of you are comfortably cruising through your lives, assuming that you will live into your 80s and have lots of time to leisurely figure these things out.

Do so at your own peril.

All of that can change in an instant with a high-speed car accident, ruptured brain aneurysm, massive heart attack, carbon monoxide poisoning, or a malignant bladder tumor that alerts you to its presence with an episode of painless bloody urination. Since you don't know how much time you have to live, doesn't it make sense to tackle life's big questions now and make the most of the unknown amount of time you have left?

Given my knowledge of statistics, probability, and patients whose lives have been cut short, I have adopted this personal strategy for living: I floss, I wear a seatbelt, and I maximize my 401K. Other than that,

I live each day as if it could be my last because I don't want to die with regrets about important work left undone. In particular, I want to make sure that I am well rooted in my purpose for living, and live that purpose every day.

A directional sign on the basement floor of the Kaiser Redwood City Hospital hammered home for me the stark reality of the brevity of a human life.

The sign was mounted to the ceiling in a hallway just outside a bank of elevators. The top line read "Birth Certificates," the bottom line read "Decedent Affairs," and the arrow pointed down the hall, to the right. My thought was that the amount of time preceding birth, represented by the space above the words "Birth Certificates," was infinite as it reached to the sky; as was the time following death, represented by the space below the words "Decedent Affairs," that reached down to the center of the earth. The minuscule half-inch space between the words "Birth Certificates" and "Decedent Affairs, that tiny parcel of signage real estate, represented the duration of a human life. Regardless of whether that life spans one day or 100 years, against the backdrop of all time, it is a brief candle, a vanishing mist, whose bookends are duly noted in an office, down the hall, to the right.

Let me take a moment for a couple of comments about the style and flow of this book…

1. I want you to feel as if we are having a conversation over a lazy outdoor lunch at a nice cafe. We are enjoying partial shade and a gentle breeze. Our server is not rushing us out, keeps refilling our glasses with refreshing beverages, and after a couple of hours, politely asks if we would like to see the appetizer and dessert menus again. I hope that this book generates invitations to meet and work together in person, so that I can be blessed by your part of the conversation.

2. Some pearls may seem to contradict one another. For example, the chapter titled "Wired at Birth" emphasizes the powerful role of genetics in human performance and is followed by "Choice Trumps Circumstances," the story of a young man who overcomes his congenital deformities to become a competitive athlete.

I encourage you to relax and just enjoy the ride. As Ralph Waldo Emerson said, "A foolish consistency is the hobgoblin of little minds, adored by little statesmen, philosophers, and divines."

Other pearls may be inconsistent with your beliefs or the theme you expect this book to have. This reflects the diverse sources of the pearls and my desire to be, like my father, inclusive and inquisitive, convicted but not convicting, principled but not prickly.

What Cornell nutritionist T. Colin Campbell says about healthy eating also applies to advice about living your best life: "There is no one answer. Rather, a symphony of solutions"

One last thing before you turn the page and start diving for pearls. It's a simple two-minute exercise in mindful breathing that I practice on a regular basis.

Find a comfortable place to sit down and settle yourself. Close your eyes. Focus on your breath. Acknowledge the inevitable distractions of your busy life, and return to your breath.

As you breathe in, be grateful that you are alive to take a breath, and celebrate the fact that for one more day, the muscle fibers in your diaphragm can fire and create a vacuum in your chest that draws fresh air into your lungs. Celebrate your alveoli, the tiny terminal air sacs that create an interface between your breath and your blood, a place where carbon dioxide exits and oxygen enters your body. Be grateful for the quiet space between your inhaled and exhaled breath, a restful pause that happens 12–15 times a minute with no conscious effort on your part.

And finally, as you exhale, let go of not only your breath, but also those things that no longer serve you well, including long-held beliefs, feelings, and behaviors that are keeping you from leading your best life.

PART I

FIRST THINGS FIRST

CHAPTER 1

WIRED AT BIRTH

(so don't take too much credit or blame for your floors and ceilings)

EXHIBIT 1: Roger Clemens, one of the most dominant power pitchers in the history of Major League Baseball, said, "Anything is possible if you have the mindset and the will and the desire to do it and put the time in." I can understand why he said that, given his personal life story, but Roger Clemens is out of touch with the huddled masses of mere mortals and wholly unfamiliar with the story of the Chuck brothers.

My brother Paul is four years older than me and he sprang from my mother's loins imbued with great balance, coordination, and a competitive spirit. If he took up a hobby or sport, he worked hard to be the best at it. The combination of his innate ability, drive, and commitment to practice produced results that were something to behold.

To watch him chase down a grounder, scoop it up and throw it across the diamond; come around a pick, get set, and shoot a basketball; swiftly position his feet, take his racquet back and swing through a tennis ball: or weave his way down a snowy mountainside with all parts of his body in sync—all of these wonderful athletic feats were nothing short of poetry in motion.

But his level of athletic achievement was not in the cards for me, his taller, slender, weaker, and less-coordinated younger brother, encumbered with not only the aforementioned abdominal pain, but also asthma. Same parents, same two sisters, same food, same three bedroom, one bath house in the Sunset District of San Francisco. Totally different athletic ceiling.

When heading down a ski slope, as soon as the speed started to pick up, my brain would scream "Pizza!"—a reminder to point my ski tips towards the midline and redirect all of my weight to the inner side of my everted feet to slow my downward descent to a certain death.

When my ninth-grade summer league baseball team made it to the city championship game and I had the opportunity to shine, I struck out swinging three times. I saw the ball clearly, stepped into it, and swung hard with my nose down, only to hear the ball hit the catcher's glove with a thud that was followed by the umpire's call of "strike three."

In case you're wondering how I compared to Paul when given the same opportunity, look no further than our relative performances on Coach Stan Smith's Lowell High School basketball teams. Paul got playing time, lots of kudos, and the girls. I barely made the team, was issued a previous-generation game uniform featuring a noticeably different fabric and font, and logged a precious few minutes of playing time and a couple of points over two seasons.

But I'm definitely not complaining. I was lucky just to make the squad, and earn the right to say for the rest of my life that I played on my high school basketball team. But just to be clear, I am no Paul, and never will be.

EXHIBIT 2: Standardized testing is another example of genetics playing a major role in performance. Have you ever known someone who barely studied for the SAT and got a perfect or near perfect score? Conversely, we all know students who have subjected themselves to multiple expensive SAT prep courses, only to suffer from a series of mediocre scores.

It has been argued that standardized testing is nothing more than a test of standardized thinking. That may be a little harsh. But it is absolutely true that such tests reward people whose brains are literally wired in a certain way.

Said the Yale-bound daughter of one of my colleagues, "Dad, when I sit down to a standardized test, I'm in my element."

Lucky her.

EXHIBIT 3: When I was a third-year family medicine resident, my medical student came to me inconsolable. Had a patient died? Did he make a mistake? Did his girlfriend leave him for a resident?

No, he had just received his blood test results, and his elevated cholesterol level had not budged even after engaging in a vigorous exercise program and eating a low-fat vegan diet for six months. Meanwhile, other medical students living sedentary lifestyles while regularly gorging themselves on cinnamon rolls, pizza, and fried chicken had remarkably low cholesterol levels.

Go figure.

EXHIBIT 4: When I entered the exam room to meet Janelle for the first time, she was already in tears. This short stocky woman clothed in snugly fitting black spandex workout clothes had just come from the gym.

She went on to describe how one year of a very nutritious and low-calorie diet coupled with a comprehensive exercise program did not budge her body mass index (BMI) which was solidly stuck in the obese range. More importantly, she did not like the way her body appeared compared to the waify models featured in magazines.

My reassurances that longevity and good health were linked more to healthy eating patterns and regular physical activity than BMI were of no consolation. She was determined to look a certain way, but that look was absent in her deck of DNA.

My point is this: we are born with genetic predispositions that can help us or hurt us in the various endeavors of our lives. Whatever our genetics are, coaching, learning, motivation, hard work, and repetition have the potential to help us perform better over time.

However, intertwined in our genetics are impenetrable floors and ceilings to how much hair we will hang on to in our old age, our swiftness of foot, and our ability to fend off the latest novel respiratory virus.

CHAPTER 2

CHOICE TRUMPS CIRCUMSTANCES

*"You can't go back and change the beginning,
but you can start where you are and change the ending."*

—*C.S. Lewis*

Talk about a rough start, Roger Crawford was born with ectrodactylism, a rare genetic disorder affecting one in every 90,000 newborns which results in the absence of fingers and/or toes. He emerged from his mother's womb with only one finger on his right hand, two on his left hand, and three toes on his right foot. Plus he was missing his left leg below the knee.

It would have been perfectly acceptable for Roger to grow up angry and depressed about his situation and to settle into a sedentary life that included work as an accountant and hobbies such as video games and spectator sports.

But when Roger saw his childhood friends playing and enjoying tennis, it looked like lots of fun, so he decided to pick up the game. Unable to grip a racquet in the traditional manner, he wedged his right finger into the open throat of a Wilson T2000 metal racquet and stabilized the shaft against his inner forearm using his two left fingers. Through a truckload of hard work, Roger went on to not only enjoy a winning high school tennis career but also earn his way onto the Division 1 tennis team at Loyola Marymount University. This was followed by a successful career as a tennis pro and motivational speaker.

It would be erroneous to say that Roger Crawford could have gone on to be a big money winner on the pro tour or that he could have wrested a few Wimbledon titles away from the likes of Bjorn Borg, John McEnroe, and Jimmy Connors. However, the courage he showed in overcoming his physical handicaps stands tall as proof that the choices we make about how we respond to our circumstances can help us become our best selves.

CHAPTER 3

THE PURSUIT OF HAPPINESS

*(Spoiler Alert: The Best Kind is Not About Things,
Circumstances, or You)*

When asked what we want most out of life and what we want for our children, a common response is "to be happy." University of California psychology professor Sonja Lyubomirsky describes happiness as the experience of frequent positive emotions (such as joy, interest, and pride) and infrequent negative emotions (such as sadness, anxiety, and anger).

Who wouldn't want that?

How do we achieve happiness? And once we have it, how can we hang onto it?

In his 2002 book, *Authentic Happiness*, University of Pennsylvania psychology professor Martin Seligman, widely regarded as the father of positive psychology, describes two main types of happiness. The first is the hedonistic happiness that we have all experienced. It is a short-term feeling of pleasure based on activities or circumstances such as hitting a home run, eating an ice cream cone, or getting an A on a final exam. The second is authentic happiness, a slow burn version of happiness fueled by discovering our strengths (such as wisdom, courage, or transcendence) and applying them to do purposeful work in the world.

When I think about these two types of happiness, what stands out is the contrast in their intent, substance, and effect. We're talking about the difference between taking the best of the world for ourselves and the giving the best of ourselves to the world; frantically filling an empty void (that turns out to be a bottomless pit of consumption) and contentedly building on bedrock a legacy that will survive us; soaking up high society and building a just society; pleasure seeking and promise keeping.

How important is finding and fulfilling purpose? In the opening line of his book, *The Purpose Driven Life*, Pastor Rick Warren writes, "It's not about you. The purpose of your life is far greater than your personal fulfillment, your peace of mind, or even your happiness."

Eli Finkel, a professor of psychology at Northwestern, chimes in with this pearl that acknowledges both hedonistic and authentic happiness, and adds his subjective ranking of the two: "Happiness is some blend of the experience of pleasure and the experience of meaning and fulfillment in life, and I think much more of the latter than the former."

I know what you're thinking: "Purpose is good and fine, but if I can just get my son into Harvard he (and we) will be set for a lifetime of happiness." And so you would think.

But that's not what happiness expert Shawn Achor discovered while a student and researcher at Harvard. It turns out that our genes, environment, and circumstances are not good predictors of long-term happiness. Legions of people bred in privilege, armed with academic credentials, and enjoying lofty titles and big incomes are very unhappy. Rather, it is the lens through which we see our reality, and the positive mindset and habits we employ on a daily basis, that drive our authentic happiness.

In my medical practice, I had the privilege of having many end-of-life conversations with patients. They would invariably talk about the joys and sorrows of their lives, a final tally of their successes and failures.

Those who enjoyed terminal happiness attributed it to deep and long-lasting relationships and work for causes they believed in. Think intact marriages featuring mutual respect and a shared commitment to work things out; parenting that models compassion, humility, and service to others; choosing work that balances making money with doing good; coaching and mentoring young people; volunteering at food banks; fostering shelter animals; and checking in regularly on an elderly neighbor. None of my patients attributed their happiness to individual achievement or the accumulation of material things.

As for regrets and failures, the most common culprits cited were not spending enough time with important people in their lives and not finding and doing the work that brought them joy.

CHAPTER 4

INDIVIDUAL ACHIEVEMENT IN A TEAM ENVIRONMENT

"Talent wins games, but teamwork and intelligence win championships."

—*Michael Jordan*

I subscribe to *The New York Times*, a newspaper founded in 1851 that has grown to enjoy worldwide readership and influence. *The Times* launched with this explanation of its purpose and position in society: "We shall be *Conservative*, in all cases where we think Conservatism essential to the public good;—and we shall be *Radical* in everything which may seem to us to require radical treatment and radical reform. We do not believe that *everything* in Society is either exactly right or exactly wrong;—what is good we desire to preserve and improve;—what is evil, to exterminate, or reform."

The Times' motto of "All The News That's Fit to Print" was coined by Arthur Ochs who assumed control of the paper in 1896. The Ochs-Sulzberger family has ruled over the media giant without interruption since that time and the results have been nothing short of industry leading with *The Times* garnering more Pulitzer Prizes (130 as of 2021) than any other newspaper (The Washington Post came in a distant second at 69).

I enjoy reading *The Times* because over many years I have come to trust the integrity of its editorial staff and the research and writing of its reporters. But how did the leadership team of *The Times* develop its winning culture over the past century? What type of people do they hire and what do they task them to do once they arrive? How do you convince thousands of individual journalists, each with their own ideas and career aspirations, to do the hard work of *The Times*?

I found the answer in a television interview with publisher Arthur Sulzberger Jr. Mr. Sulzberger said that *The Times* recruited and hired talented journalists who wanted to achieve great things not only for themselves but also to advance the mission of *The New York Times*. In saying this, he was acknowledging the natural human tendency to strive for individual achievement and recognition.

At the same time, he was notifying candidates that it was imperative that their individual achievements contribute to a much bigger picture of excellence in journalism. As a person who understood how the small picture of winning games fits into the big picture of winning championships, he was intentionally creating a culture of individual achievement in a team environment.

It's a win, win, win game for individual journalists, *The Times*, and those who turn to *The Times* for a better understanding of the facts and how those facts fit into the context of our lives.

CHAPTER 5

CONNECTION

"The currency of wellness is connection"

—John Travis

W hile earning his medical degree at Tufts, John Travis became disillusioned with the disease-focused model of medical care and became interested in the drivers of wellness. Influenced by the work of John Halbert Dunn (often referred to as the father of the modern wellness movement and author of *High Level Wellness*) and armed with both a master's degree in public health and a preventive medicine residency at Johns Hopkins, Travis opened the world's first wellness center in Mill Valley, California in 1975.

His focus on inspiring people to be well, rather than treating illness, steadily gained traction, followers, and media attention, including a 1979 visit from Dan Rather and his *60 Minutes* crew.

The association of wellness with connection, and unwellness with disconnection, makes intuitive sense. In his book *God's Voice Within*, Mark E. Thibodeaux describes in detail the desolation of isolation versus the consolation of community. Something deep within all of us yearns for linkages to a world beyond ourselves.

What are the specific types of connection that promote wellness?

The answer is found in Richard Swenson's *Margin: Restoring Emotional, Physical, Financial, and Time Reserves to Overloaded Lives*. Like me, Dr. Swenson is a family physician who has listened to countless patient stories about personal pain and suffering. He concludes that a major reason for personal unwellness is that people are looking for wellness in the wrong places.

He preaches that wellness comes not from the prevailing pursuit of things, but rather from three types of relationships. The first is the relationship we have with other people in our lives, which he refers to as our social life. The second is our relationship with ourselves, which he calls our emotional life. This relationship includes our thoughts and the stories we tell ourselves about ourselves. Lastly, he defines the relationship we have with God as our spiritual life. I would add that many of us also derive happiness from our relationship with nature. Think hiking in a national park, snorkeling in Hawaii, and star gazing. I call this our Grizzly Adams life.

I learned this valuable life lesson about relationships early in my career from an elderly gentleman who was a patient on our hospital's hospice service.

He was not a regular patient of mine, but I was taking care of him for a colleague on the weekend. After I chatted with him for a while and performed my examination, I asked if there was anything I could do for him. He politely replied "No," but asked if he could share some advice with me, a young doctor fresh out of training. "Please do," I replied.

He looked up at me with his sunken eyes, and said with great deliberation and deep love, "I just want to let you know, that at the end of your life, all you have left are your relationships." #micdrop

CHAPTER 6

LISTEN MORE, TALK LESS

"We have two ears and one mouth
so that we can listen twice as much as we speak."

—Epictetus

Connection is the currency of wellness and communication is the primary way we connect with one another. Thus the popularity of communications courses and consultants who promise to teach us the secrets of effective speaking, writing, listening, and hearing.

Public speaking aside (because it's a weighty topic that deserves its own books and workshops), the primary purpose of speaking in communication is to demonstrate hearing and understanding. When we demonstrate that we are sincerely curious about another person's thoughts, opinions, and feelings, as well as how they came to hold them, we win trust and respect, and pave the path for an ongoing mutually productive relationship. Teddy Roosevelt put it this way: "People don't care how much you know, until they know how much you care." Nothing shouts, "I care!" louder than being a good listener.

Dr. Rachel Remen, a pioneer in the mind/body holistic health movement and the founder of a popular *Finding Meaning in Medicine* program for healthcare professionals, speaks about the power of replacing what she calls "listening with judgement and comparison" with a more generous listening style. Generous listeners refrain from asking:

25

"Do I agree with it?"

"Do I like it?"

"Is it accurate?"

"Do I like this person?"

When we listen with this intent and restraint, people are free to tell us what really matters to them and what gives them meaning. In this regard, generous listening is a gift we give to others and ourselves.

> *"If you listen closely, the patient will tell you the diagnosis."*
> —*Dean Sherman Mellinkoff, UCLA School of Medicine*

Similar intentions can be found in Dr. Terry Stein's patient-centered *Four Habits Model* of physician-patient communication. While the four habits were designed for doctors working with patients, the principles apply to numerous types of communication encounters outside of medicine.

The first habit is to quickly establish rapport and to set the stage for the encounter. In the doctor-patient scenario, this might look something like this:

Doctor: "Welcome Mr. Chan. How can I help you today?"
          —accompanied by a warm handshake and good eye contact.
Patient: "It's nice to meet you Dr. Johnson. I'm here today because
          I have a headache."

The second habit is to solicit the patient's perspective of the problem. This is distinctly different from the patient's *chief complaint*, which is the headache.

What the physician really wants to discover is the *chief concern* about the headache. What about the headache is worrying the patient and prompted him to seek further evaluation? A common chief concern in this scenario would be that the patient's relative had a similar symptom that was "ignored" by their doctor, and it turned out to be a brain tumor.

For that reason, the patient wants to see a neurologist and get a head scan as soon as possible.

The third habit is to demonstrate empathy. Empathy is the ability to understand the feelings and perspectives of another human being. According to Brene Brown, empathy brings people together and involves perspective-taking, staying out of judgement, recognizing emotion in other people, and demonstrating understanding. It is feeling *with* people.

"I can understand why you are scared about the possible causes of your headache. What your Auntie Mae went through sounds so upsetting and tragic."

This as opposed to sympathy, which is based in pity and sorrow for someone's misfortune and drives people apart. While sympathy often comes from a good place, its expression often comes off as awkwardly dismissive and out of touch with the pain of the sufferer.

The fourth habit is to invest in the end. The details of this closing step will vary depending on the specifics of the encounter but the following three elements are commonly employed by physicians who are effective connectors and communicators.

Summarizing the encounter: "It was nice to meet you today. You started out by telling me about your headache and what I heard you say is that your greatest concern about your headache is that it might be caused by something dangerous like the brain tumor you Auntie Mae had. Based on your answers to my additional questions and the results of my physical examination, I think that you most likely have what is called a muscle tension headache, not a brain tumor."

Involving the patient in joint decision making: "Based on my diagnosis, I have a plan for how to treat your headache. I'm going to email you a link from my physician home page that describes muscle tension headaches in greater detail. After you read it, let me know if you have any questions. Follow the guidelines for treatment and then send me a progress report. If your headache persists or changes in any way, be sure to let me know so that I can decide if you need further evaluation and testing. What do you think of this plan?"

Closing the visit with a question: "Do you have any questions about our plan?" This allows the patient to air any remaining concerns. While asking this question may seem like an invitation to the never-ending visit, not asking it will invariably lead to follow up emails, phone calls, and appointments—so best to ask sincerely on a regular basis.

CHAPTER 7

FRIENDS FOR THE JOURNEY, INCLUDING PALLBEARER BUDDIES

"A journey is best measured in friends, rather than miles."

—Tim Cahill

In her book *Friendfluence*, Carlin Flora describes the many benefits of having friends, including learning how to get along with others, sharpening our minds, defining our priorities, setting goals, discovering where we fit in society, meeting our romantic interests, sharing life's ups and downs, and being happier in general.

But how do we choose and make friends? Do opposites attract or do birds of a feather flock together? In a *Journal of Personality and Social Psychology* article titled, "Similarity in Relationships as Niche Construction: Choice, Stability, and Influence Within Dyads in a Free Choice Environment," Angela Bahns and Chris Crandall report that future friends or partners are already similar at the outset of their social connection. "You try to create a social world where you're comfortable, where you succeed, where you have people you can trust and with whom you can cooperate to meet your goals," Crandall said. "To create this, similarity is very useful, and people are attracted to it most of the time."

While there are advantages to clustering in like-minded circles of friends (add comfort, familiarity, and harmony to those listed above), the downside is that it leads to a smaller life with far fewer opportunities for fresh ideas, stimulating conversations, and new adventures.

My personal experience with developing a group of close friends largely unlike myself is one of chance rather than intention. The "Fairfield Poker Group" was started 30 years ago when a small group of first-time moms met one another through an infant play group. Their husbands, including me, started a monthly poker game. I was a family physician of Chinese descent, a registered Democrat, and a flag waiver for liberal causes. The majority of the group were white Republican businessmen who believed in small government. But these differences made no difference during our gatherings. All of us were just glad to get out of the house to enjoy a few beers and win or lose a few bucks.

Over many years, the group settled into a steady stable of eight regulars—Brad, Jamie, Dave, Gene, Rick, Pat, Dave, and me—and we added to our regular game an annual weekend away in the mountains or the coast. We grew closer and attended many of one another's important social events including weddings, baby parties, and birthday celebrations.

At one point a few years ago, for no one particular reason that I can remember, I suggested to my wife, Lesli, that perhaps it was time for me to step away from the poker group. It was probably a combination of things that led to this change of heart: another political text string; a comment meant to be humorous but perceived by me as off-color; or maybe I had simply lost more money than usual the night before.

Plus I could never really keep up with our group's alcohol consumption (many Asians lack the aldehyde dehydrogenase enzyme required to metabolize alcohol, resulting in the facial flushing known as "the Asian glow") and my Honda Accord looked puny compared to their Hummers and Mercedes.

Lesli listened to my tale of woe, paused, and then replied, "You might want to consider what you would lose by leaving the poker group."

My initial reaction was that she did not want my withdrawal from the group to interfere with her corresponding night out with her girlfriends.

But her opinion was rooted in concern about my welfare, not hers. She went on to share a piece of advice that I treasure to this day: "If you were only friends with people who were just like you, you would have no friends."

I immediately realized that Lesli was absolutely right about that. Even if I could find friends who were just like me, how incredibly dull would a meeting of such homogenous minds and bodies be? Answer: super dull, verging on deadly dull.

It turns out that the differences between my poker friends and me have actually served to fill many of my gaps in perspective and experience. Here are some examples of how they have helped me lead a more comprehensive and informed life:

1. They have shown me that in addition to tax-funded social welfare programs, a substantial way to show love for our fellow citizens is to build strong businesses that provide people with jobs, good salaries, and benefits. This in turn allows those employees to provide for their families, support causes they believe in, and live out their personal and professional dreams.

2. They have shown me that people who support candidates and political parties I disagree with are not all stupid or evil. In fact, they want most of the same things I want for America and its people. In the end, they just believe in a different way to get there.

3. They have shown me that loyalty to country and a heart for helping others takes many shapes, many of which I am unfamiliar with, but eager to learn more about.

4. Thanks to them, I know a lot more about business, the stock market, sales careers, taking a company public, casinos, golf, boats, fishing, liquor, red wine, and world travel.

5. They have shown me that friendship has the power to supersede differences of background and opinions.

In the end, my poker group of mostly dissimilar friends has been a big plus in the ledger of my life. For many years now, I have called them my pallbearer buddies, meaning that when I die, I know that they will be there to look after my family and carry my casket or urn at my memorial service. That's how close I feel to them after 30 years of playing cards, drinking beer, inhaling snack foods, and sharing many laughs, burps, and farts.

An invitation I received from Jamie's daughter, Jennifer, and her fiance, Martin, to officiate their wedding served as evidence of the depth of our friendships and its extension to our families. The ceremony was held in the courtyard of a beachfront resort in Santa Barbara. The Pacific Ocean served as the perfect backdrop for the couple's nuptials and the weather was perfect—sunny with a slight breeze.

As I led the couple through their marriage vows, I looked over to Jamie, who was seated in the front row box seats reserved for the father and mother of the bride. He was beaming with joy. His rugged good looks, dapper tuxedo, and love for his family and friends propelled him past George Clooney as the most handsome and content man in the world. In that moment, I knew for certain that my enduring friendship with the poker boys, my pallbearer buddies, was one of the greatest blessings of my life.

CHAPTER 8

A Strategy for Winning

"Hope is not a strategy."

—Anonymous

In his NPR program titled, *How I Built This*, host Guy Raz interviews the founders of many of the world's most well-known companies such as Instagram, Southwest Airlines, and Patagonia. After soliciting what is always a refreshingly vulnerable story filled with risk taking and setbacks, his final question is, "How much of your success do you attribute to luck, or just hard work?" The answer is usually something along the lines of a 50:50 split. One could argue that hard work creates opportunities that could be interpreted as good luck.

The truth of the matter is that if you look at the inner workings of individuals and organizations that are successful over the long term, the key element of success is neither hard work nor luck. It is strategy. Strategy is an action plan for winning. It's something that Napoleon, John D. Rockefeller, and Bill Gates had in spades and that Oprah Winfrey has leveraged to earn the title, "Queen of All Media."

Early in my leadership career, I had the pleasure of attending a seminar on strategy taught by Robert Burgelman, the Edmund W. Littlefield Professor of Management at the Stanford Graduate School of Business. Professor Burgelman conducts research on the role that strategy plays in firm evolution. He makes a living by helping CEOs gain and maintain control of their destinies.

His good counsel helped our large multispecialty medical group make a historic pivot shift from being the cost leader to the quality and service leader. I remember his presentation lasting about three hours and including multiple diagrams. The distilled version of his presentation went something like this: "Strategy is having what it takes and doing what you say." By that, he meant that you must first define what winning means for you.

In the case of our medical group, we defined success as being the industry leader in access, quality, service, and cost. As for having what it takes to get that done, our competitive advantages in the marketplace were our integration and exclusive contracting with the Kaiser Permanente Hospitals and Health Plan, our information technology capabilities, our people, our culture of innovation, and our track record of visionary physician leadership.

If you are having a hard time being a consistent winner in your space despite working very hard, perhaps it's time to step back and ask yourself, "What are we trying to do with our company?" "Do we have what we need to get the job done?"

No doubt these are the fundamental questions that Bill Walsh and his coaching staff revisited over and over again as they led the San Francisco 49ers to multiple Super Bowl victories. Ditto for the Apple product development teams that have dominated the domestic cellular phone market with multiple generations of iPhones.

CHAPTER 9

More "and," Less "but"

A surefire way to kill conversations and squash budding relationships and opportunities is to overuse the word "but." "I see what you are saying Bob, *but*...." Even if it's not meant to be, the word "but" can be perceived as dismissive of the ideas, opinions, and perspectives of others. At its worst, "but" is intended to shut someone else down and clear the way for you to take center stage.

An elegant way to acknowledge the ideas of others while still getting in your two cents is to use the bridge word "and." "I understand what you are saying Bob, *and* I'd like to share a way that we could see this through an alternative lens."

CHAPTER 10

MAKING PRETEND DECISIONS

Decision theory is the study of how choices are made to achieve a goal. Some choices, such as what to wear to work and what to eat for lunch, are relatively easy. Other decisions, such as career choice, whether to marry (and if so, whom), and what you believe about a higher power, are much more difficult because the stakes and uncertainty are high.

Fear of regretting our choice, also known as buyer's remorse, adds another layer of angst and complexity to decision making. The risk of this is higher when we are presented with multiple opportunities from which to choose, and there is no clear front runner. Ambivalent types who tend to see everything as a shade of gray, struggle more than most to make a choice.

An effective way to reduce or eliminate buyer's remorse is to make a preliminary decision prior to the decision deadline—and to shop it around with family and friends.

My wife, Lesli, calls this "making a pretend decision." Coming out to your besties, parents, and Auntie Carol that you have chosen to attend Gonzaga instead of the University of Washington gives you a taste of what it feels like to be a member of your new tribe—and also gives you a sneak preview of how others will respond to your choice.

If living with your pretend decision continues to feel right after several days of floating it with others, then make it your final decision. If it doesn't feel right, figure out why and reconsider your choice.

CHAPTER 11

NOBODY'S LOOKING AT YOU

Excessive self-consciousness, and its friends embarrassment, guilt, and shame, are pebbles in our shoes that keep us from being our best selves. For that reason, it's best to drop them all like the bad habits they are.

I learned this important lesson from my wife after returning home from another one in a series of $17 haircuts at my local barbershop. I settled into my usual post haircut routine which was to park myself in front of a mirror to critique all the things that were wrong about it.

Sideburns uneven, not enough taken off the top, cowlick misman-agement resulting in hair sticking up on the back of my head. This was usually followed by questions to God about why he didn't bless me with overwhelming good looks that would transcend bad haircuts and even baldness.

After tolerating this childish behavior for a couple of decades, Lesli inquired, "Why worry about a few hairs out of place? Others are con-cerned about how they look, not so much about how you look."

Similarly, Dr. David Sobel, one of my colleagues with decades of experience in public speaking, shared his secret for overcoming stage fright. Early in his career, he assumed that his entire audience was in-tently listening to him and that he had to be at his best to win their favorable reviews. After decades of working with audiences of all types and sizes, he came to the realization that at any given time, one-third of his audience was listening to him, another third was nodding off, and the final third was thinking about sex.

Bottom line: don't take yourself so seriously that you get all stressed out and perform worse. While it is true that some people are trying to pay attention to you, for the most part, they are distracted by more interesting options.

PART II

THE WORK WORLD

CHAPTER 12

WHY YOU NEED MONEY

Life is expensive, so we need some money to pay for the things that help us survive, live, and pursue our dreams. While a small percentage of us have investments, savings, or trusts that generate a steady stream of income with little or no effort, the overwhelming majority of us need a job to meet our financial obligations.

I grew up the fourth child of a minister, and in our household there were few to no discussions about money, why it's needed, and how to earn it. However, I quickly learned that if I wanted to buy baseball cards and candy on my own, I had to have money. Picking up a friend's paper route on occasion and sweeping the sidewalk at church on Sunday mornings gave me a taste of how good it felt to earn a few bucks for spending money. In high school, I landed the sweet spot job: scooping ice cream at the local Baskin Robbins 31 Flavors shop. For $2.25 an hour, I not only earned money, but also made customers happy and ate as much ice cream as I wanted while on the clock.

Budgeting is the process by which we balance our expenses against our income. Housing, food, clothing, transportation, internet, cell phone, child care, insurance, charitable giving, vacations, gifts for family and friends, savings, taxes…the list of expenses that eat into our bottom line is lengthy.

When we can't afford what we want, we make things happen now by taking out loans, lots of them. The personal debt load of Americans totals $14 trillion—which averages out to $90,000 per person. For younger people, education loans and credit card debt are the main culprits. As we get older and settle into homes to raise families, we take on home mortgages. The goal is to pay off our debt as adults and start saving for retirement, though that remains an elusive goal for many.

CHAPTER 13

WHY PEOPLE PAY YOU

I learned the big picture of why people pay you when I worked for a startup company in the late 1990s. Our business model centered around online marketing via a virtual sales representative. One of my co-workers had earned his MBA at UCLA and arranged for a few of us to meet with his mentor, Alfred Osborne.

Professor Osborne is the founder and director of the Price Center for Innovation and Entrepreneurship and his presence fills a room. Tall and distinguished looking, with a baritone voice that delivered words of wisdom in steady measure, he told us this fundamental truth about business: people will pay you for your product or service if it solves a pressing problem that they either cannot or do not want to take care of themselves.

The corollary to this principle is that when investors are deciding which startups to fund, one of their primary considerations is whether the company offers a unique product that solves a big problem that is looking for a cost-effective solution.

Whether you are seeking your first job, trying to build your reputation where you are, or looking for new opportunities elsewhere, remember this important principle about why people pay you. Tailoring your attitude and skillset to make yourself a more competitive candidate and colleague will literally pay off for years to come.

CHAPTER 14

WORK HARD, BE KIND

Judy Davis is a legendary primary school educator and leader in the college town of Davis, California. She was the principal of my daughter Kelly's elementary school and her final year of work before retirement was Kelly's graduation year. At the graduation ceremony, the parents were eager to hear what she had to say in the final speech of her distinguished career.

I was expecting something lengthy, perhaps a trip down memory lane highlighting her many accomplishments and fond memories that spanned over three decades.

But true to her selfless personality, she walked up to the microphone and said that this day was not about her, but the graduating students. She said she had four words of advice for the sixth graders as they made the transition from elementary school to junior high, words that would serve them well for the rest of their lives: "Work hard, be kind."

To this day, I cannot think of four words that provide better advice for the work world and life. Work hard, because hard work is virtuous, is what employers expect from you, and inspires those around you to step up to the plate and do the same. Be kind, because intentional kindness builds relationships, trust, and camaraderie—and makes the workplace and this world a better place for everyone.

CHAPTER 15

SHOW UP AND FOLLOW THROUGH

"Between the idea and the reality,
between the motion and the act, falls the Shadow."

—T.S. Eliot, The Hollow Men

My in-laws live in a nice subdivision of Fair Oaks, a comfortable suburb of Sacramento located fifteen minutes east of the state capital on the way to the gold country and Lake Tahoe. One of their neighbors and close family friends was Dave Cox, an insurance salesman who rose through the political ranks to become a two-term Republican State Senator. Dave was a barrel of laughs. At our wedding reception, he was the guy parked by the beer keg sharing funny stories with an appreciative audience.

Dave succumbed to prostate cancer during his second Senate term and our family attended his funeral service at the Cathedral of the Blessed Sacrament near the Capitol building. From our seats in the rear balcony, we witnessed a parade of elected officials and dignitaries, including then-Governor Arnold Schwarzenegger, file into the sanctuary to pay their respects.

Among the scheduled speakers was Dave's Chief of Staff, Kevin Bassett, who told a story that illustrated how Dave leveraged showing up and following through to become a popular and effective leader.

Residents of Amador County contacted him to complain about noise from hay trucks coming down a highway near their homes. You can imagine how another elected official might have assigned an intern to contact the constituents to gently remind them that the freeway was there before the homes were built, and that the most effective solutions to the problem would be to grow tall hedges and upgrade to double-paned windows.

Dave Cox was not that guy.

At 4 a.m. the following morning, he gathered up his staff and drove one and a half hours to meet the local highway patrol commander to listen to hay trucks. Why? Because Dave cared about people and understood that showing up and being present with people made them feel respected and valued.

If showing up is the perfect appetizer, following through is the satisfying and often elusive main course. Dave deftly sidestepped the "shadows" that keep many of us from turning our ideas into reality and motions into action—shadows such as fear of failure, perfectionism, procrastination, and just plain laziness.

Perhaps it was his part-time job at a mortuary during college that taught him things need to be done right, on time, and with a deep sense of responsibility to the client. His commitment to getting back to people and helping them with advice and legislative action earned him multiple public service awards and the respect and admiration of his constituents.

Jack Mitchell summed up his feelings about Dave in this *Amador Ledger-Dispatch* editorial titled, "Making Government Work for the People": "I remember recently calling on behalf of a local business that needed some assistance. Instead of lip-service, or passing the buck, Senator Cox invited us to visit him at the State Capitol. He listened to the problems this new business was having, quickly gave an overview of who they needed to talk to and then told them who he was going to contact on their behalf to make sure everything was taken care of.

"As we were leaving the Senator's office, the business owners, who had never met Senator Cox before said, "This guy is like Mr. Smith goes to Washington. I mean, he's really one of us.

"And if there was any doubt in their minds about Senator Dave Cox, they were quickly eliminated the next day when they received phone calls from everyone that Senator Cox said he was going to contact on their behalf, including a call from the Senator's staff to make sure they were pleased with the outcome.

"This was a common occurrence with Senator Cox and his office staff. I don't know how he juggled all the items, or how he found time to do everything he needed to, but he got it done."

CHAPTER 16

BE FLEXIBLE & LEARN HOW TO
GET ALONG WITH OTHER PEOPLE

When my son graduated from UCLA with a bachelor's degree in Communications, the commencement ceremony was held in majestic Royce Hall, a twin-towered brick and tile building that has become the trademark image of the university.

The guest speaker was UCLA Communications alumnus Jorge Garcia, best known for his portrayal of Hugo "Hurley" Reyes in the television series *Lost*. Of note, he also played a drug dealer on *Curb Your Enthusiasm* in 2004 and had a recurring role as conspiracy theorist Jerry Ortega in the updated version of one of my childhood favorites, *Hawaii Five-0*.

Jorge was born in Omaha, Nebraska to a Chilean father and Cuban mother. He grew up to be a big boy, topping out at six feet tall and a few hundred pounds. No doubt this created some employment opportunities and excluded others. Like all actors, he auditioned for many parts, endured many rejections, and survived by adapting to a wide range of unpredictable circumstances and mercurial producers, directors, and co-stars.

His advice for my son and his fellow graduates setting out to navigate the world was this: *"Be flexible and learn how to get along with other people.*" Why flexible? Because the world is a dynamic place, and we must adapt to its constant changes to get things done. The alternative, being rigid and uncompromising in the face of new realities, is a recipe for frustration, discouragement, and failure. Being pliable when necessary, like the claymation star, Gumby, allows us to bend without breaking, both day-to-day, and over a long career.

Getting along with people is a mighty tall order, and is the subject of many books, seminars, and coaching and counseling careers. These are five steps that will get you off to a good start:

1. Be friendly

2. Be humble. By this I mean think more of others and be less preoccupied with yourself.

3. Try to understand the feelings of other people

4. Look for win-win scenarios where everyone on the team comes out ahead

5. Respond to perceived indignities and slights by repeating steps #1–4

CHAPTER 17

CREATIVITY

Creativity has been defined as the act of turning original and imaginative ideas into something novel and valuable. It's a highly desirable commodity in the work world because it gives birth to new products and services and infuses positive energy into a company's culture and brand. Apple comes to mind as a hotbed of creativity, with its cutting edge, user-friendly line of personal electronic products.

Most of us don't think of ourselves as especially creative because we don't paint like Picasso, write like Maya Angelou, or revolutionize commerce like Jeff Bezos. However, in his 2005 Stanford graduation speech, Apple's Steve Jobs shared some thoughts about creativity that broadened its definition, thereby allowing more of us to be members of the club.

He said, "Creativity is just connecting things. When you ask creative people how they did something, they feel a little guilty because they didn't really do it, they just saw something. It seemed obvious to them after a while."

Case in point: midway through my career I was asked to create a mentoring program for our new hires in adult medicine, a rapidly growing department composed of general internists and family physicians. I was partnered up with Susan Helvick, a nurse and seasoned healthcare administrator. We did the usual due diligence of scouring the literature for best practices in mentoring and surveyed other departments within our medical group to find out what they were doing to help their newest physicians make a smooth transition into our multispecialty group practice.

In the latter stages of our program development, we felt that the program needed something novel to make it something better than just a compilation of existing best practices. Thinking back to my onboarding experience 10 years earlier, I felt that a missing link was a comprehensive didactic lecture series that would bring primary care physicians up to date on the specialty problems that they would commonly encounter in their practice.

Up until that time, it was customary to bring in outside speakers from academic medical centers to deliver such specialty talks. After all, weren't all of the "best" doctors practicing at UCLA and Stanford?

The answer is yes and no.

Might a UCLA professor of urology be the world's expert on a rare condition? Absolutely yes. However, they are less likely to have a broad practical knowledge of their specialty, and the volume of patients they see over a career is typically much lower than that of a community-based physician.

That's why many physicians will tell you that the most practical and applicable knowledge they acquired during their medical school and residency training came not from university-based faculty members, but from faculty based at Kaiser Permanente, an organization that cares for 12 million patients nationwide, practices evidence-based medicine, and boasts some of the best clinical outcomes in the world.

For that reason, I chose to have the teaching faculty for our new hire lecture series come exclusively from our own medical group. Not only did this expose our primary care physicians to the specialty problems they routinely encounter, but it also introduced them to the specialists they would be working with for years to come.

The mentoring program and associated lecture series turned out to be a solid success and was recognized with one of the medical group's top awards. But at its core was not the sort of creative genius that discovers new mathematical theorems or launches a new school of mixed-media art. It was simply an exercise in connecting the dots and giving top billing to an idea whose time had come.

CHAPTER 18

CALENDARS & CHECKLISTS

Many years ago, we invited our nephew to a party to be held in his honor at our home. Due to the party prep time and guest list, we asked him to mark the date and time on his calendar. He replied that it was unnecessary.

"I'll just remember," he said. He was a stellar student, so we just figured he had a clever way of keeping appointments without using the usual tools the rest of us rely on.

Fast forward a few weeks. My wife and I had prepared a nice meal and the guests had all arrived, but there was no nephew in sight. After waiting over an hour for him to show up, we called him. He told us that he had forgotten about the party—and lived too far away to make it in a reasonable amount of time.

Sound familiar? If you are having trouble keeping appointments and getting things done on time, by all means keep an electronic calendar and checklist that you can access from your home, office, or on-the-go.

I keep one calendar that includes work and personal events as well as things I want to get done that day. I prefer using an electronic calendar because I can access it from anywhere and anytime using my smartphone. I check it at night before going to bed and set alarms for important events the next day.

If I need to drive somewhere, I set the alarm for the time I need to get in my car to arrive at the appointment on time. For important virtual meetings and phone calls, I set my alarm for 3–5 minutes before the encounter, so that I can gather my thoughts before signing on or calling in.

When I wake up in the morning, I have a general idea of my schedule but double check my calendar to confirm. As my day evolves, I recheck the calendar several times and try to knock out "to do" items such as scheduling a dental appointment, following up with a friend, or buying a hair catcher for our shower drain.

Items that I don't get done by the end of the day I move to the next day, or the day I think I can complete the task.

If I have a really important project that needs to get done by a certain date, I'll put a reminder in my calendar a few days or weeks before it's due, depending on how much time it will require to complete.

For those of you who prefer to maintain a paper calendar and "to do" list, be sure to carry it with you at all times and take photos of it every now and then (in case you lose it).

As for my nephew, if we ever throw him another party, I'll be sure to remind his wife about it.

CHAPTER 19

UNIVERSALLY WANTED AND ADORED

For seven years, I was responsible for recruiting and hiring physicians for our medical group. I pored over written applications, called references, and conducted hundreds of in-person interviews. In the end, I hired 250 physicians. Since I also had oversight for our mentoring program and performance evaluations, I was able to evaluate how my hires panned out in the workplace.

What kind of worker and colleague was I looking for? Pretty much what every employer is looking for in a candidate: a person with integrity, a strong work ethic, and a commitment to working with teammates to get the job done for clients (in our cases, patients).

In addition to the usual interview questions, I asked candidates the following:

"On a scale of 1–10 with 1 being 'my life is all about me' and 10 being 'my life is all about others,' where are you now and what direction are you going?"

"When things go bad (as they are bound to do), after a brief period of appropriate complaining, are you part of the problem or part of the solution?"

Their answers to these two questions were important, but the purpose of asking them was twofold. First, I wanted to forewarn them that a career in medicine sometimes calls on us to make personal sacrifices for the benefit of our patients. Second, I wanted to make it perfectly clear that we were recruiting for problem solvers who could help us achieve our goal of providing high quality, personalized care, not complainers who would sit back and make snide remarks from the peanut gallery.

My work in recruiting and hiring led me to ask people from all walks of life about what they were looking for in employees and co-workers. I have distilled their comments into these three traits that define high performers in a wide variety of work settings:

1. A demonstrated capacity for hard work

2. The ability to make progress amid chaos

3. A commitment to be part of the solution

In short, if you work hard, achieve success even when circumstances are not ideal, and are a team player, you will maximize your chances of being hired and enjoying a very successful and satisfying career.

PART III

LOFTY GOALS

CHAPTER 20

GOING PUBLIC OR SERVING THE PUBLIC?

David Talbot is a San Francisco-based author and activist. In 1995 he founded Salon.com, a liberal web magazine covering U.S. politics, culture, and current events. The magazine enjoyed immediate success and *Time Magazine* named Salon.com its website of the year.

After leaving Salon.com, Talbot wrote a series of best-selling books including *Brothers* (JFK's administration and Robert Kennedy's investigation of his brother's assassination), *The Devil's Chessboard* (Allen Dulles' transformation of the CIA), and *Season of the Witch* (the decline and rebirth of my hometown, San Francisco).

In 2015, disturbed by what he believed to be the cultural demise and gentrification of many of San Francisco's historically working-class neighborhoods, Talbot delivered a scathing speech at Stanford University, located just 40 minutes down the peninsula from his home. He scolded those in his audience who would use their talent, power, and influence for harmful and selfish pursuits, and their newfound wealth to transform formerly funky and eclectic communities such as his own Bernal Heights enclave, into playgrounds for Tesla-driving techies.

Said Talbot, "This is what it comes down to…Are you interested in going public, or in serving the public—that's the fundamental question a Stanford student has to ask these days. When I was in college, we had a saying—'You're either part of the problem or you're part of the solution.' Which one are you?"

As much as this Cal graduate is tempted to twist Talbot's knife further into the belly of those affiliated with "The Farm" (Stanford's nickname rooted in the university property having previously served as Leland and Jane Stanford's livestock farm), I would say that this question about going public or serving the public is something that all of us must ask ourselves, at all stages of our lives. Will the two-minute synopsis of your life serve as a case study in toxic individualism, or as an inspirational example of compassionate collectivism?

CHAPTER 21

Breaking Away from the Thundering Herd

"'I have the right to do anything,' you say—but not everything is beneficial. 'I have the right to do anything'— but not everything is constructive.'"

—1 Corinthians 10:23

In America, the rallying cries of the horses in the thundering herd are individualism and materialism. We may worship God with song and hands raised to heaven on Sunday, but what we hold most dear the rest of the week is the right of the individual to say and do what we want to achieve personal fortune and fame.

While there are practitioners and pockets of humility and modesty in our society, they pale in comparison to the pervasive culture of "me" and "look at me."

It's as if we believe the person who dies with the most toys and awards wins the game of life. But the stories my patients have told me at the end of their lives, about their greatest achievements and most profound regrets, build a much stronger case for looking beyond ourselves for meaning and the satisfaction of a life well-lived. In the final box score of human life, deep relationships and making a positive difference are the only stats that matter. Things are but a footnote and mean nothing, especially if you have no one to share them with.

Adds Yale's Bryan Garsten, in a nod to the ancient teachings of Plato, "Allowing our desires to grow always larger is like spending our lives trying to fill a sieve, or welcoming a lifetime of itchiness so that we can always have the satisfaction of scratching ourselves again."

Still, it's hard to overcome inertia and the prevailing culture. How do we break away from the thundering herd, get out of a race we never asked to be in, and settle into a lane that takes us where we want to go?

The first step is to decide that we don't like the trajectory of our current curve. If you find yourself on the alluring path of a lucrative career spent diverting money from the poor to the rich, see relationships as a means of increasing your personal fortune and popularity, and like the person you are becoming through such pursuits, by all means, forge ahead. Ditto if you believe that abandoning your commitments to people and causes that rely on you is what you need to do to live your best life.

But if you come to realize that repeatedly focusing on yourself and your happiness is leading to an existence short on meaning and purpose, change directions and break away from the thundering herd. The first thing you will notice is how quiet it is, and how for the first time in a long time, you can hear your inner self speaking to you.

The next step is to find your new herd. Seek out or reconnect with the people and causes that speak to what you are trying to achieve with your life. As you scan the horizon, you will see groups of all shapes and sizes roaming the plains. Dust off your hooves, muster up some courage, and run with those that appeal to you to sample their rhythm, cadence, and direction.

The goal is to find a herd where with relatively little effort, you glide into their slipstream and experience a state of complete and utter immersion that psychologist Mihaly Csikszentmihalyi calls "flow." In Csikszentmihalyi's words, flow is "a state in which people are so involved in an activity that nothing else seems to matter; the experience is so enjoyable that people will continue to do it even at great cost, for the sheer sake of doing it."

You will like flow.

Members of the thundering herd will be confused by your pivot shift, and will pepper you with questions and comments such as, "How could you walk away from so much money?" and "You're too smart to be a community organizer."

But rest assured that your life's journey will be filled with wonderfully rewarding experiences and relationships. And in the end, you will die with authentic joy and few regrets.

CHAPTER 22

BENDING THE CURVE

My family has a love affair with the University of California at Davis. It was founded in 1909 as the University Farm School and served as an outpost for faculty and students from UC Berkeley's College of Agriculture. Over the next 100 years it grew by leaps and bounds into a comprehensive major research university with its affiliated professional schools.

My wife, her three siblings, and our daughter are all alumni and I did my residency at the UC Davis Medical Center in Sacramento.

I had the pleasure of serving as UC Davis Foundation trustee for eight years. This Foundation's primary job was to raise funds to support the work of the university. Most of the trustees were grateful UC Davis alumni who wanted to give something back to their alma mater. The university welcomed our money, influence, and good ideas.

I remember one brainstorming session in which the trustees were asked to come up with slogans for an upcoming major fundraising campaign. Based on my prior educational experiences at two older and more established UC campuses, UC Berkeley and UCLA, UC Davis stood out to me as being an especially friendly place. So I lobbied for a slogan that went like this: "UC Davis: where excellence, kindness, and you come together to change the world."

Someone else pitched "UC Davis, we touch everything that matters in life," a slogan that referenced UC Davis' broad reach in numerous areas that affect our daily lives—such as agriculture, engineering, and veterinary medicine.

But the idea that I liked most came from fellow trustee Guy Benstead, an investment advisor who earned a degree in International Relations from UC Davis and then an MBA from Columbia. Guy's suggestion was "At UC Davis, we're changing the trajectory of the human race."

Guy was making a bold statement that for over a century, the collective efforts of the UC Davis family were powerful enough to positively influence how mankind experienced life on planet earth and beyond, and that this was a train worth boarding for the ride of a lifetime.

I'm not sure if I or any team I work on will ever come close to changing the arc of history. But I would hate to get to the end of my life and regret that I never tried.

CHAPTER 23

PAINT THE PICTURE-PERFECT POSTCARD

There's no way you will achieve great things without some planning. And since you only live once, you might as well shoot for the stars. If you come up short, you will have still gone a long way, and you will forever enjoy the satisfaction of giving a big dream your best shot.

One way to put your moonshot idea to paper is to create the "picture-perfect postcard" of your destination. No need to dumb it down with "buts." Just go crazy, as if there were no limits to your imagination, talent, and resources. Picture in your mind what your destination looks like. Shoot for perfect, and be very happy with a supreme effort that gets you partway there. And just to stay focused, make your postcard big enough to include all of its essential elements, but not so large that it is encumbered by extraneous distractions.

Walt Disney's vision for what became Disneyland is a good example of a picture-perfect postcard. Unsatisfied with amusement parks where kids played while adults sat on benches, he envisioned a theme park where both the parents and children could have fun. This simple but profound vision grew into what many consider "the happiest place on earth."

In 1961, President John F. Kennedy shared his picture-perfect postcard vision of safely landing an American on the moon before the end of the decade. In 1969, Apollo 11 and its crew of three astronauts did just that, setting up Neil Armstrong to utter these famous words: "That's one small step for a man, one giant leap for mankind."

UCLA's Paul Terasaki had a picture-perfect postcard vision that transplant specialists could one day easily identify optimal matches between organ donors and recipients. The problem was that there was no quick and easy way to determine if a recipient's immune system would reject the donated organ through a complicated process that is orchestrated by the major histocompatibility complex (MHC), a segment of human DNA that determines how an individual's immune system distinguishes self from potentially dangerous non-self invaders.

Dr. Terasaki developed a microcytotoxicity assay which required only tiny amounts of blood to determine an individual's human leukocyte antigens (a subset of the MHC). Using results of HLA typing, doctors could match up donors and recipients with similar HLA profiles, thereby minimizing the likelihood of organ rejection. In essence, Dr. Terasaki invented HLA speed-dating.

CHAPTER 24

VALUES-CONGRUENT LIVING

Along with a team of physician colleagues, health educators, and a psychologist, I co-developed and taught a one-and-a-half day evidence-based physician resilience course. My colleagues did most of the heavy lifting. I liked to joke that I was the team's eye candy.

Using experiential learning, we gathered small groups of my colleagues (approximately 20–30 at a time), paired each participant with an accountability partner, and taught them how to integrate the habits associated with good health and well-being into their daily lives.

In the audience were practicing clinicians from all specialties. Their ages ranged from the early 30s to the late 60s. The course started with one of my teaching partners walking the audience through an inventory of their personal values and having them use the results to begin writing a personal mission statement.

After a short break, I led a module on developing social networks and imitating resilient others. As part of my welcoming comments, I would ask the bridge question, "How many of you have done a personal values inventory and written a personal mission statement before today?" Over many years, the percentage of affirmative replies ranged from 15 to 25 percent. Never 50, 75, or 90 percent. Always one quarter of the class, or less.

My tongue-in-cheek explanation for the low percentage goes something like this: while everyone else in college was smoking marijuana and backpacking in Europe figuring out the meaning of life, pre-meds were busy studying calculus, chemistry, and biology and preparing for the MCAT exam.

For that reason, physicians as a group are behind their non-physician peers with regards to thoughtful introspection and the development of mission statements. No wonder that physician burnout rates hover around fifty percent.

Research has shown that people who lead values-congruent lives in which they are pursuing their life missions are more resilient and happy. But what are values and what is a values-congruent life?

Values are the deeply held beliefs that we hold to be fundamentally good, desirable, and important. They embody what we stand for, how we want to behave, and what we want to do with our lives. We experience values-congruent living when our thoughts and actions reflect our beliefs and the trajectory of our existence is headed towards our ideal self.

Our values express themselves in numerous domains including work, family, spirituality, health, leisure, and engagement with our social networks, community, and environment. Examples of values are providing for family; being a good parent; taking care of our environment; knowing, loving, and serving a higher power; and being a reliable friend.

One of the main benefits of defining and prioritizing our values is that it allows us to develop a personal mission statement for our lives. That statement serves as a compass and trail guide that helps us to make decisions when we are confronted with choices about how to think and what to do.

An example of a personal mission statement is, "My mission is to be an extraordinary mother, spouse, and leader in my organization. I want to be compassionate with others and inspire those around me."

You can see how putting this mission into words would help an individual make important decisions such as whether or not to accept a job transfer to a distant city or stay in a marriage that has lost its emotional energy.

CHAPTER 25

BENEVOLENCE

Benevolence: The disposition to do good; good will;
charitableness; love of mankind, accompanied with
a desire to promote their happiness.

—Webster's

My father, James, was a gifted student and lifelong learner. I think that his deep curiosity about things unfamiliar to him was his way of making up for a relatively sheltered upbringing by Chinese-speaking parents who did not venture much outside of San Francisco's Chinatown.

After graduating Phi Beta Kappa from Cal with a degree in psychology, he earned his doctorate of theology while working as a minister and nominally helping my mother to raise my three siblings and me.

What I remember from my childhood was that when he wasn't working or playing catch with me in front of the house, he was reading, meeting with people who needed help, or teaching himself something new, like conversational Mandarin.

His greatest gift was his ability to develop a thorough understanding about a complicated topic and then distill it to a simple message that people from all walks of life could understand. He would spend days researching a sermon topic, develop a story that brought the message to life, and then preach from brief notes that he scribbled on the back side of an envelope.

Forty years after hearing it, I still remember a sermon he gave about benevolence. I don't recall the specific scripture passage that he cited. It might have been Proverbs 25:21 ("If your enemy is hungry, give him bread to eat; and if he is thirsty, give him water to drink") or James 2:26 (faith without works is dead). Either way, the message of his story was that "benevolence is wanting for other people's children what you want for your own."

This type of benevolence goes far beyond being kind and charitable to a peer in need. It is an extraordinary act of love that begins with digging deep into your belief system and defining the essential values, skills, opportunities, and possessions you want your children to have so that they can survive and thrive.

What comes next is the game changer. You work for other people's children to have the exact same things. You evolve from being a legacy hoarder to a legacy sharer. In doing so, you give the next generation a big head start on living together in harmony.

CHAPTER 26

MR. WILLIAMS' WISH

My daughter Kelly's high school graduation ceremony was held at the school's football stadium on a late afternoon in June. The dark green artificial turf had absorbed scorching heat all day and became a giant outdoor Easy-Bake Oven for the students, faculty, family, and friends who had gathered for this quintessential adolescent rite of passage.

Students stayed cool by wearing shorts, t-shirts, and flip flops under their rented vivid blue gowns and passing around spray bottles and wet towels. As a family physician, I was certain that I would be called into action to tend to an elderly grandparent succumbing to heat exhaustion or a student passing out from alcohol intoxication.

As was the custom, the students selected a favorite faculty member to give a speech. That year they chose Kevin Williams from the social studies department.

The city of Davis is home to a highly ranked University of California campus, so Davis High is very much a college prep school, filled with high achieving students with ambitions to attend prestigious universities and make their mark on the world. For that reason, I expected Mr. Williams to deliver a speech outlining the tips and tools the students would need to distinguish themselves as top-tier performers and leaders in school and the work world.

But on this day, as sure as I was hot and sweaty, I was dead wrong.

Mr. Williams' unexpected and refreshing message went something like this: "My heartfelt wish for you is that at some point in your life, you will have the opportunity to work with other people for a cause greater than yourself."

In a "me" world, on a day that was all about "me," he was planting a seed in the graduates' minds that life offers something bigger and better than individual achievement and recognition. He was sharing this wisdom of the elders with the Young Turks: life is best lived in community, and the best way to gain access to what is big, important, and meaningful in life is to join hands with others, launch bodacious ideas, and embark on courageous adventures that change the world for the better.

CHAPTER 27

WE NEED MORE MINGAS

For centuries, the peoples inhabiting the highlands of Columbia, Ecuador, Peru, and Bolivia have achieved big things by calling for a minga. A minga is a volunteer collaborative effort to do something positive for the community. Mingas leverage the power of teamwork to achieve what otherwise could not be done by individuals or small groups of people. Mingas construct irrigation systems, repair roads, and rebuild villages after fires.

The North American version of a minga, common in the 18th and 19th centuries, was barn raising, a community project in which neighbors came together to construct a barn over several days. Most of the foremen and laborers were volunteers, and there was an expectation of reciprocity between neighboring farmers. You help me now, and you can fully rely on me to help you later.

When I consider the major problems facing our world, problems such as global climate change, maldistribution of wealth, overpopulation, food insecurity, and pandemics, I'm thinking that we need a minga mentality to face them head on. No more responding to challenges by blaming others and sowing seeds of division.

Let's put aside our differences, find some common ground, and come together to build some barns.

CHAPTER 28

KIVA LOVE

Jessica Jackley is the co-founder of Kiva, the world's first person-to-person microlending website. The mission of Kiva is "to expand financial access to help underserved communities thrive." It works like this: ordinary people like you and me can go online to kiva.org and loan money to low-income entrepreneurs and students in seventy-seven different countries. The experiment is working. To date, 1.9 million lenders have funded 3.8 million borrowers to the tune of 1.5 billion dollars. The repayment rate is 96 percent.

What kind of person launches such a powerful benevolent nonprofit organization that simultaneously helps people align their spending with their social values and gives hope to the hopeless in faraway lands?

Ms. Jackley grew up in the small borough of Franklin Park, Pennsylvania. After completing her undergraduate studies in philosophy and political science at Bucknell University, she earned her MBA at Stanford.

Instead of following many of her classmates to lucrative Silicon Valley jobs, she broke away from the thundering herd and followed a path that led to Kiva, as well as subsequent endeavors related to growing social entrepreneurship, philanthropy, and cultivating a civil society.

When asked by a fellow MBA alumnus whether she regretted not choosing a more traditional and financially lucrative business career, she replied, "No, because I'm rich in the currency that is meaningful to me."

For Jessica Jackley, the currency that was meaningful to her was being part of the solution on pressing issues such as social equity, financial literacy and independence, and the redistribution of opportunity.

What currency is meaningful to you? What types of pursuits and achievements fulfill your purpose in life?

If we want to save our planet and the human race, we need legions of Jessica Jackleys choosing to use their smarts, connections, and influence for causes that are bigger and better than the individual pursuit of money and fame.

CHAPTER 29

THE MORAL BUCKET LIST

The best opinion piece I have read in the past ten years comes from David Brooks. It is titled "The Moral Bucket List" and was published in *The New York Times* in 2015. Brooks describes a morally good person as, "one of those incandescent souls you sometimes meet," someone who is always doing good for others and never thinking about himself.

He suggests that those special people are rare exceptions because our society and culture emphasize the attainment of resume virtues over eulogy virtues. We hotly pursue the diplomas, certificates, and skills that make us shine in the work world and help us climb the social ladder. Conversely, we make meager efforts to develop the attitudes, behaviors, and habits that are talked about at our funerals and memorial services—virtues such as kindness, bravery, honesty, faithfulness, and love. Failure to correct our moral trajectory results in "a humiliating gap" between ourselves and those incandescent souls we aspire to be.

A traditional bucket list is composed of the experiences and achievements we want to have during our lifetimes. But the more disconnected these lists are from our ultimate purposes, the more likely we will be left feeling unsatisfied and unsettled even after all the boxes have been checked.

Another option is to start by defining our destinations ("incandescent soul" comes to mind as a good choice). Then work backwards to fill our lives with the experiences and achievements that will get us there.

I know an incandescent soul and his name is Alan Anzai. Alan is younger and more fit than me, so I will probably be too dead to share my respect and admiration for him at his memorial service.

So I will do it now.

Alan attended the Saint Louis School in Honolulu where his father, a career Air Force officer, was his track coach. In his senior year, Alan was crowned Hawaii's boys cross country state champion with a three mile time of 15:45.0. He ran track and completed his pre-med studies at the U.S. Air Force Academy. This was followed by medical school at Loma Linda University (where he earned Alpha Omega Alpha academic honors), a family medicine residency at Kaiser Permanente Fontana, and nine years of military service in California and Japan.

For some people, such stellar resumes are the result of self-centered pursuits and the basis for a lifetime of boasting. But for Alan, the resume achievements are more a measure of his commitment to develop his mind and body for a lifetime of service to country and community. For that reason, you could work side-by-side with Alan for ten years, and never know that he was a track star, Air Force Academy graduate, a member of AOA, and a veteran who served his country, because he would never tell you.

Alan joined The Permanente Medical Group in 2004 and quickly established a reputation as an excellent clinician and soft-spoken leader.

He also had a penchant for understanding personal finance and sharing his knowledge with colleagues. He wasn't offering buy and sell recommendations. Rather, he was coaching people to live financially responsible lives. "Want what you have rather than work to have what you want" and "Compare yourself with people who have less (and share what you have with them) rather than compare yourself with people who have more (and covet what they have)" are two Alan Anzai finance pearls that I have adopted for myself.

Alan and his wife Shing also walk the talk. They live in a comfortable but modest home, drive sensible cars, and give generously of their time and resources to support their church and safety net medical clinics (and I suspect numerous other causes that they are too modest to mention).

Several years ago there was an opportunity to run for an open position on our medical group's board of directors and all shareholders at our medical center were welcome to apply. The nominating committee selected from the applicants a slate of four candidates that included Alan and me, and the two of us ended up in a runoff to determine who would serve on the board.

As we were waiting for the runoff votes to be tallied, Alan called to wish me luck and confided that he had voted for me to win. Who does that? An incandescent soul who is kind, selfless, and loving, that's who.

Despite casting his vote for me, Alan won the runoff, and in my estimation, he has proven himself to be one of the most hard working and effective board members in the history of our medical group. In addition to helping to orchestrate a successful CEO transition and being a tireless advocate for our patients and colleagues, he is putting his financial sensibilities to good use by chairing our retirement committee.

CHAPTER 30

AUTHENTIC HUMILITY

Courtney Jimenez was the best female athlete I ever watched perform at Davis High School. I base that assessment on my observation of her performance at the annual powder puff football game that pits the senior class women against the juniors. Her sport was soccer, but in this particular game she was playing flag football against women from multiple sports including basketball, field hockey, lacrosse, volleyball, and softball. Her acceleration, speed, shiftiness, and vision were on full display that day as she sliced through the opposition in a way that I have only seen in one other athlete: DeSean Jackson when he was playing football for Cal and then the Philadelphia Eagles.

Courtney was also a top student, and that combined with a presence and poise beyond her years made her a natural born leader. She stayed in town to attend UC Davis and participated in the College Life fellowship group affiliated with the First Baptist Church of Davis. College Life's weekly meetings were held on campus on Tuesday evenings and featured worship music and a lesson that was delivered by our church's college minister, a College Life advisor, or a student.

When I found out that Courtney was scheduled to speak, I made it a priority to clear my work schedule and get to the meeting on time, knowing that the venue would be packed. Sure enough, I barely got a seat in a very crowded Storer Hall. The room was abuzz with excitement about what Courtney would say. She did not disappoint.

Her topic was humility and she drew her message from Philippians 2 which reads, "Therefore if you have any encouragement from being united with Christ, if any comfort from his love, if any common sharing in the Spirit, if any tenderness and compassion, then make my joy complete by being like-minded, having the same love, being one in spirit and of one mind. Do nothing out of selfish ambition or vain conceit. Rather, in humility value others above yourselves, not looking to your own interests but each of you to the interests of the others."

Humility is a difficult subject to understand and embrace, and college students have an additional barrier to adoption. As humble as they would like to be, college is the time for them to distinguish themselves as smarter, faster, stronger, funnier, and more attractive than their peers for the purposes of earning good grades, awards, friends, and whatever else they need to get where they want to go.

The teachings of Jesus and his apostles set high standards that fly in the face of our prevailing individualism and materialism. Which left Courtney's attentive audience in a tough spot, having to choose between what feels familiar and necessary (self-confidence and self-achievement) and what God is calling them to do ("in humility, value others *above* yourselves").

Courtney addressed the tension with a reminder that authentic humility is not thinking less about yourself; it is thinking more about others. This refreshing reframe provided her audience with an opportunity to temper tendencies to compete and compare with a newfound curiosity about other people's lives—and a heart for encouraging them in their pursuits of knowledge, truth, and meaning.

CHAPTER 31

JOY

"Joy is the gosh darn beautiful
hum of contentment in your chest."
—*Dr. Animesh Sinha*

UC Davis sponsors an annual book project to promote dialogue and build community by encouraging diverse members of the campus and surrounding communities to read the same book and attend related events. For the 2018–2019 academic year they chose *The Book of Joy*, Doug Abrams' account of a five-day audience he had with His Holiness the Dalai Lama and Bishop Desmond Tutu.

Mr. Abrams' question for these two world leaders, both admired for their steadfast good works in the face of persecution was, "How can we find joy amidst the suffering of the human experience?"

Mr. Abrams came to the campus' beautiful Mondavi Center for the Performing Arts to talk about the book and its message. My wife and I had the pleasure of hearing him speak from a pair of cozy seats in the right rear of the orchestra section. He shared many stories from the two men, and identified three themes that ran through all of them.

The first is that joy is not the same as happiness. Happiness is a feeling based on circumstances. You are happy because you got a raise at work or your child was recognized for her achievement in sports. Joy is a choice. You choose it and its presence in your life is independent of what is happening around you or to you.

The second is that joy is inseparable from suffering. They are two sides of the same coin, and that coin is called life. So stop waiting for the absence of suffering to find your joy.

The third is that the greatest joy of all comes from bringing joy to others, regardless of whether you are having or feeling joy yourself. This is the principle that allowed His Holiness and the Bishop to continue their good works regardless of their circumstances.

CHAPTER 32

LEAVING YOUR MARK

Glen Snyder was the Senior Pastor at the First Baptist Church of Davis for many years. A former high school basketball standout and avid adult golfer, he was a no-nonsense, Bible-based preacher, and always at his best in times of crisis.

I remember getting an early morning phone call from a friend who was experiencing acute personal distress. I'll call him Colin. The particulars were all bad and I didn't know what to say, so I told him that I would meet him for lunch to find out more and offer whatever support I could.

After hanging up the phone, I realized that I had no idea what I would say or do at lunch to be helpful. So I immediately called Glen to ask for advice. Glen calmly provided this good counsel: "By all means, don't tell him that this is God's will and that things will be fine. Rather, hear him out and validate that this is a horrible situation—and that perhaps in five to ten years from now he might be able to see God's hand in what happened."

I followed Glen's advice and showed up to lunch with the sole intention of being a good listener for Colin. After hearing more of the particulars, the only appropriate response was for me to say, "I'm so sorry. This is horrible. I am here for you." Fast forward ten years: things worked out beautifully for my friend. The moment of crisis turned out to be a very favorable turning point in his personal life and the entire experience helped him and his family to grow their faith in God.

I wondered whether Glen's gift for helping people in crisis was something that came naturally to him or if he had intentionally trained for it. The answer to my question was revealed during one of his Sunday sermons.

He recounted a conversation he had as a young seminary student with one of his mentors. The professor advised Glen that it is important to help prepare a congregation for suffering. For even if they were not suffering at the time, they would certainly experience suffering in the future. The mentor also advised him to be "a deep and long-lasting positive influence in the community you serve."

Mission accomplished Glen. Thanks for doing just that for so many people in their time of greatest need.

CHAPTER 33

MEANING

We say that we want to have meaningful lives, but what is meaning? This is one word where dictionaries do not provide much guidance.

Dr. Rachel Remen provides an answer that I find to be satisfying. Her *Finding Meaning in Medicine* groups and courses help healthcare professionals reconnect to their meaning. Decades ago, her observation was that healers found solace and satisfaction when they gathered in small groups to share personal stories about what made their work worthwhile. It all started as an experiment in which she invited a few doctors to her home to talk about their experiences. She provided the tea and cookies. Story themes varied and included fear, courage, compassion, boundaries, loneliness, and dreams. Through their sharing and receiving of stories, attendees emerged feeling more connected to themselves and others.

As a wellness leader in my medical group, I wanted to find out more about Dr. Remen and her message so I signed up to attend her two-and-one-half-day "Rekindling the Flame" workshop. The venue was the Mills Park Hotel, located on the main drag of Yellow Springs Ohio, a village of 3500 people one hour west of Columbus. Born, raised, and educated in California, I saw this as the perfect opportunity to both immerse myself in the Midwest for a few days and sit at the feet of the medical community's meaning guru.

Yellow Springs was a pleasant change of pace from California. The home to Antioch College and comedian Dave Chappelle, it provided a welcome relief to the more densely populated and fast paced communities to which I was accustomed. It struck me as the idyllic place to raise a family and be a teacher or coffee shop owner.

About 50 people signed up for the course. My classmates included physicians, nurses, social workers, and educators from throughout the country. We all had one thing in common: we were feeling disconnected from the meaning of our work and wanted to learn how to get it back.

Motivated by my personal burnout and pain, I brought to the class a tremendous desire to soak up Dr. Remen's wisdom. I had not noticed in myself this degree of thirst for knowledge since my first year of medical school 35 years prior. I took a front row seat near the center aisle, just a few feet from the speaker's slightly elevated stage, notebook open, pen to paper.

Shortly after she began to speak, I could not help myself and raised my hand to ask, "Dr. Remen, what is meaning?"

I wish that the moment had been recorded so that I could review what happened next. But my interpretation of her reply is something you would find in a script from the television series *Kung Fu*, starring David Carradine as the young Shaolin monk, Kwai Chang Caine, and Keye Luke as his mentor, Master Po: "Patience young grasshopper."

Message received.

During the last half hour of what was an insightful and inspiring journey of intuitive and experiential learning, Dr. Remen finally articulated her definition of meaning.

"Meaning," she said, "is the deep satisfaction of knowing that you matter, and that what you do makes a positive difference in the lives of others and the world around you." Yet another #micdrop moment in my personal wellness and meaning journey.

CHAPTER 34

THE TRIFECTA

"Trifecta appeared in the early 1970's as the name for a horse racing bet in which the first, second, and third place winners are chosen in the correct order. More recently the word has broadened in meaning to include the clustering of three very desirable things."

—paraphrased from Merriam-Webster

Like clockwork, my father would turn to my mother around 9 p.m. every evening and say to her, "Fun gow" (Cantonese for sleep) as he headed to their bedroom in his white Jockey briefs and t-shirt to lay his body to rest.

After a night of sleep apnea and loud snoring, he would rise up at 5 a.m., overflowing with energy and intention, and head downstairs to a modest space in the back of our garage, near the water heater and clothes dryer, that served as his home office. There, in quiet solitude, he would stand in front of a former workbench, jerry-rigged MacGyver-style with cardboard and masking tape creations (his best approximations of store bought storage units and desk organizers), and knock out a couple of hours of solid work before heading out to his day job at The First Chinese Baptist Church in San Francisco's Chinatown.

My dad's morning rallying cry, which he often said out loud for the world to hear, was "I'm grateful for meaningful work and the strength to do it." This powerful proclamation of thanks established a positive tone for the rest of his day. His gratitude filled him with energy to read another book in his vast library, write essays, sermons, and personal letters, and learn new languages.

And it was the perfect prelude for venturing out into the world in his gold Toyota Corona sedan to partner with his associate pastor, staff, and lay leaders to care for their congregation and community.

In this simple but powerful way, James made the most of each day by leveraging a trifecta of three blessings that no one should ever take for granted: meaningful work, the strength to do it, and an audience to do it with, and for.

CHAPTER 35

"I'LL JUST RENT"

The terms low, middle, and upper class are based on the median income. Those earning $0 to 66% of the median income are defined as lower class; from 66% to 200% of the median income are the bookends for the middle class; and anything over twice the median income is considered upper class.

I grew up in a lower middle income household. Our family had plenty to eat, clothes to wear, a modest but comfortable home, and enough money to buy a new Chevrolet or Toyota sedan every eight to ten years. Our vacations consisted of church camps and visits to relatives in Fresno or Los Angeles.

I remember small allowances as a child, but it was clear to my three older siblings and me that we had to work part-time jobs in junior high and high school if we wanted spending money. Our college education options were the local community colleges and public universities, and the latter was only affordable if we could secure state grants and scholarships.

UC Berkeley and the UCLA School of Medicine afforded me the opportunity to get a top-notch education at bargain basement prices, and set me up for a career in medicine where I could be of service to others while earning an income that exceeded that of my parents.

My wife and I raised our family in an upper middle-class neighborhood in a university town. We provided for our children the most memorable opportunities and experiences of our childhoods, and then working within our budget, supplemented that with some entertainment, dining, and vacation experiences that we did not have growing up.

My son Tyler was a well-rounded high school student. He excelled in the classroom, made the tennis team, played piano in the jazz band, and was elected student body president. He inherited a gift for music from his maternal grandfather, and he was in his element when he sat down to play the piano using a "fake book" composed of the basic chords from jazz classics.

Based on his broad skill set and academic abilities, I thought Tyler would make a good pediatrician. I figured that he could survive the premed, medical school, and residency grind, take care of sick kids during the day, and use his earnings to support his family and love of music.

I made arrangements for him to shadow pediatric colleagues in the outpatient and hospital settings, and sent him off to college where I assumed he would take the required pre-med courses and apply to medical school.

Tyler headed off to UCLA but it was not long before he stopped taking pre-med courses. He found many of the students in those classes to be more competitive and less friendly than the people he met in his social science classes.

I told him that this was just part of the pre-med personality, and that these same people would evolve into compassionate healers after being admitted to medical school. He didn't buy that. Come to think of it, the constant striving and desire to seek advancement and recognition in medicine never really ends. Shame on me for living in denial and trying to sugarcoat that distasteful underbelly of a medical career.

"Do not lay up for yourselves treasures on earth, where moth and rust destroy and where thieves break in and steal, but lay up for yourselves treasures in heaven, where neither moth nor rust destroys and where thieves do not break in and steal. For where your treasure is, there your heart will be also."

—Matthew 6:19–21

Tyler found a major that interested him, Communication Studies, and discovered that he had a passion for teaching. Through Teach for America, he taught special education at Richmond High School in the San Francisco Bay Area for three years, and then transitioned into his current nonprofit education work that focuses on strengthening science teaching and learning for elementary and middle school children in underrepresented minority and low-income communities.

Ever the concerned parent, I have spoken with Tyler about potential career pivot shifts and higher paying work that would give him a fighting chance of purchasing a home in one of America's most expensive real estate markets.

He has politely endured these overtures while making it clear that he is not interested in making more money or pursuing material comforts. He says that his empowerment is rooted in purposeful work that addresses the educational needs of people in communities that are otherwise largely forgotten. In that regard, he has already achieved Jessica Jackley's goal of being rich in the currency that is meaningful to him.

As for buying a house, it's not on his radar. "I'll just rent," he says.

CHAPTER 36

GREATNESS REDEFINED

"Anyone who wants to be first must be the last,
and servant of all."

—*Mark 9:35*

If you are reading this book in order you already know that I'm a huge fan of my father James and his teachings. But James was not one to toot his own horn, post on social media, or write a book to ensure that his wisdom and teachings survived him.

Enter his grandson Evan Lessler, the creative founder of Adapt Clothing, a successful retail business that features aesthetically pleasing concepts printed on clothing and accessories.

Evan took the audio recording of my father's sermon from September 24, 2006 titled "Greatness Redefined" and married it to images and background music. You can find it on YouTube and it is nothing short of three minutes and fourteen seconds of pure gold.

Says James, "Greatness is not just something about yourself. It's not about what you can accomplish, but greatness has everything to do with what you do for other people and what you mean for other people. Whoever wants to be first must be last of all, and servant of all. Jesus, in this particular text, completely redefines our understanding of greatness. It is not about yourself, but it's about what you mean to other people and the way you enlarge and bless the lives of others.

"It's not about me and how successful I am, and it's not about how much money a person like me through my ingenuity and my smarts can make.

"It's about how I spend my life to make the lives of other people better.

"The world is full of people you never hear anything about who are doing significant things to enrich and enhance the lives of other people. And some of them are people you know: single mothers that are trying to raise their children; people who are making tremendous sacrifices to help their aging parents; people doing all sorts of things who will be greatly missed when they are no longer in the land of the living.

"Think about your own life. How little there is of it. How precious every moment is. And how you like me, we have choices about what we are going to do with that life.

"Everybody has to die sometime. So the tragic thing about life is not that we have to die. The tragic thing about life is wasting it. You don't want to waste it. Wasting your life is the worst thing you can do.

"When people see the 2,000-word version of your life, it has meaning. Everything fits in. The disappointments end up turning our lives in certain really good directions. Jesus, counterculture, understanding of what our life is about."

PART IV

GETTING THINGS DONE

CHAPTER 37

A FRAMEWORK OF
ENERGY AND CHAPTERS

What is the context in which we get big things done in our lives?

In its performance optimization courses for high performance athletes and business executives, whom it generously refers to as "corporate athletes," the Human Performance Institute teaches its students how to most effectively get things done by managing their energy. Their pyramid of energy domains begins with a broad base of physical energy and graduates in ascending order to include emotional, mental, and finally, spiritual energy.

In the physical realm, the goal is to maximize energy through optimal movement, nutrition, and sleep. The emotional work focuses on building self-confidence and building healthy relationships. Mental focus is improved through mindfulness and the prioritization of the work that matters most. And finally, spiritual enlightenment is achieved through aligning values with work (described in Chapter 24 as values-congruent living). The "incandescent souls" David Brooks speaks of in his previously mentioned essay about the moral bucket list are good examples of people who have reached the summit of the energy pyramid.

In his book *Falling Upward, A Spirituality for the Two Halves of Life*, Franciscan friar, teacher, and author Richard Rohr provides a working framework that helps us to name and navigate two essential chapters of our life story and better understand the timing and intentions of each. These are the stages of life in which we manage our energy.

The first half focuses on the individual hard work and achievement that earns us access to many of the things we want to get our life going on the right track: educational opportunities, employment, a life partner, and a reputation as a human being worthy of respect and support.

A successful first half prepares us to transition into the second half in which the focus shifts from "me" to "we". In this second half, we are in a stronger position to commit to relationships with people we love and causes we believe in. Building on a foundation in which our basic wants and needs for survival and happiness have been met, we have the capacity to pursue some of the lofty goals described earlier such as serving the public, bending the curve, and engaging with others to work for causes greater than ourselves.

Life can be problematic if we fail to move beyond the first half of life. For many, there are major socioeconomic barriers that make the transition difficult, if not impossible.

However, our ranks are filled with people of means who intentionally choose to be permanent residents of the first half of life. They have no lofty goals beyond the next job promotion, incentive bonus, or number of "likes" on their latest social media post. Their lifelong pursuit of individual achievement and recognition invariably leads to despair and loneliness.

The only hope for those who choose to take up permanent residence in the first half? When they hit rock bottom, and then that bottom gives way, an incandescent soul will be there to catch them.

CHAPTER 38

TAKE CHARGE

Maria Ansari attended the University of Michigan for college, medical school, and her internal medicine residency and then headed west to UC San Francisco for her fellowship in cardiology.

She currently serves as the Physician-in-Chief at the Kaiser San Francisco Medical Center. In that role she oversees hundreds of physicians taking care of several hundred thousand patients.

Like most of the physicians in our large multispecialty group practice, she derives her primary joy and meaning from direct patient care. Yet, she also understands that steering our medical group's ship requires some clinicians to step up and assume executive leadership roles. In the final analysis, her decision to take the plunge was influenced by this advice from a trusted mentor: "If you are getting motion sick at the back of the bus, get up and drive."

I love that call to action for so many reasons beyond its imagery. First, it reminds us that passively enduring chaos in our lives is miserable. We've all been there, unhappy with our circumstances, but unable or unwilling to muster the energy to do something about it. Second, it is a rallying cry to make the transition from follower to leader, a transition that empowers us to see the world through a different lens, one that views problems as opportunities to effect positive change.

Who are you at work, in your family, and in your community? Are you the employee who never volunteers to be the leader or offer up an alternative solution, yet you have plenty of time and energy to criticize everything the leader does? Are you the family member who never plans the summer vacation but then complains about the rental house and takes the best room? Are you the citizen who incessantly complains about government yet never gets involved in civic life?

If you answered yes to these questions and often find yourself saying, "They should have done this…" maybe it's time for you to stop complaining and start doing.

I get it. It's hard to declare yourself a leader. You become a lightning rod for the criticism you are so accustomed to dishing out. But it's also hard sitting in the back of the bus getting sick.

I'll let you choose your hard.

CHAPTER 39

LEAD FROM WHERE YOU STAND

One of the most common misunderstandings about leadership is that one needs a formal position and title of authority to lead. Strictly speaking, leaders are people who get others to follow, and for this, no position or title is required.

Case in point: Carlos Bustamante was the head custodian at our medical office. His official job responsibility was to keep our facility clean and tidy, a critically important job for so many reasons, including the fact that nothing earns a patient's confidence faster and more powerfully than a spotless and pleasant-smelling lobby, restroom, waiting room, and exam room.

But Carlos brought that and so much more to the operations and culture of our team. He came to work every day with unbridled energy and a commitment to serve others. He had a bounce in his step and an ever-present smile on his face that filled the space around him with positive energy.

If I was having a bad day and he walked into the room, I would feed off of his energy and feel better. If he could maintain his professionalism and good cheer while cleaning up blood, pus, and vomit, I could try to do the same while running behind on my schedule or being berated by a patient.

Carlos also led all of us in the building to be more physically fit. He took a brisk midday walk during the lunch hour and inspired many of us to do the same. While there was always a temptation to stay at our desk and work through lunch, we noticed that Carlos always returned from his walks refreshed and invigorated to take on his afternoon work.

Sure enough, whenever I pried myself away from my computer and phone to get outside, breathe some fresh air, and get in my steps, I always returned to the office with a boost of energy and newfound enthusiasm to serve my patients that afternoon.

If Carlos was such a powerful leader in his role as custodian, you can similarly lead others in a way that transcends your official title and role. Doing so will both build your reputation among your peers as a leader and will also increase your chances of earning a formal leadership role.

CHAPTER 40

Use What You've Got

Jason Aldean is a country music star with numerous #1 hits. Says my friend and pastor Dan Seitz, "He's the everyman of today's marquee country music stars. He doesn't have the guitar-shredding ability of Brad Paisley or Keith Urban, the Texas Stadium filling charisma of somebody like Kenny Chesney, the soulful baritone rumble of Darius Rucker, or the song-writing chops of Eric Church. Compared to those high wattage stars, he's the energy efficient bulb. He knows this and reflects on it in his song, 'I Use What I Got.'

> *I use what I got*
> *Take what I get*
> *Until I ain't got nothin' left*
> *Then I give it some more*
> *Keep on climbing up that mountain*
> *Keep truckin' along, work up a sweat*
> *Past every "no" after "no" after "no" till I get a "yes"*
> *I don't worry about what I've done*
> *I use what I got, yeah.*

"Jason Aldean declares that rather than fretting about what he doesn't have, he is determined to use what he's got to press ahead."

CHAPTER 41

EXCELLENCE

Francis Frei and Anne Morris are founders of The Leadership Forum which exists to help more and varied leaders be successful.

In their *Harvard Business Review* article titled, "Culture Takes Over When The CEO Leaves the Room," they share their world view that excellence = design x culture. Design includes strategy, business models, and incentives. Culture consists of the shared values, belief systems, and expectations of discretionary behavior when dealing with issues not found in the employee handbook.

At the medical office where I worked, physicians took turns being the leader of the adult medicine team, usually for a period of three to five years. I had the good fortune of taking over from a colleague who was very detail-oriented. She had cultivated binders of information about our office's plan for optimal operations. This created an opportunity for me to focus on the culture that would make her hard work come to fruition.

I reminded our team members that at Kaiser Permanente, we valued our prepaid model of evidence-based care and believed in an integrated system where the insurance company, hospitals, and healthcare professionals worked together to provide high-quality personalized care. These fundamentals positioned our organization to be the best place to work and the best place to receive care.

As for discretionary behavior, there was only one rule: do for our patients what we would want done for ourselves. This simple approach empowered everyone on the team to take ownership of the work and to be a problem-solving leader.

For this reason, I never worried about how any of my teammates treated a patient or colleague when the CEO left the room.

CHAPTER 42

Servant Leadership

Leaders are people who get other people to follow them. The best leaders get people to follow them under challenging circumstances that include VUCA (an acronym coined by the US War College in 1987 to describe the volatility, uncertainty, complexity, and ambiguity that followed the dissolution of the USSR).

Author Bruna Martinuzzi describes the seven main leadership styles as autocratic ("Do as I say"), authoritative ("Follow me"), pacesetting ("Do as I do"), democratic ("What do you think?"), coaching ("Consider this"), affiliative ("People come first"), and laissez-faire (the opposite of autocratic). No one style fits all people or problems to be solved.

That being said, the servant leadership model championed by Robert Greenleaf stands out as a hybrid that is both intellectually and emotionally robust and applicable to a wide variety of situations. During his 38-year career with AT&T, Greenleaf came to realize that large organizations run by power reliant leaders often failed to meet the needs of individuals or society. He also observed that the most effective leaders were those who served the needs of the organization *and* the people who made that organization go.

Six years after he retired from AT&T, he wrote an essay titled, "The Servant Leader." He argued that the best leaders saw themselves as servants first and foremost, and that these people were exceptionally good at listening, persuasion, language, and focusing on metrics that mattered.

As opposed to the traditional power reliant leadership model in which the company's spotlight is on the leader, the employees are tools, and customers are challenges, Greenleaf's servant leaders redirect the focus to the employees doing the work. In this new paradigm, the customers are valued allies and the leader's job is to inspire and equip.

Here are some examples of servant leadership in action on the big stage:

Exhibit #1: John Riccitiello is a business executive who has worked at such high profile companies as Clorox, PepsiCo, Haagen Dazs, Wilson Sporting Goods, and Sara Lee.

This fellow Baby Boomer earned his business degree from the Haas School of Business at UC Berkeley in 1981, a time when a top down, "command and control" management style was the norm. Our generation believed that individuals were to be subservient to the company, and that individual success was earned through company loyalty, self-sacrifice, and paying dues over an extended period of time.

From 1997–2004 Riccitiello was the president and then chief operating officer of EA Sports, a developer of blockbuster sports video games such as Madden NFL, FIFA, and NBA Live. His workforce was made up largely of young software engineers. These Gen Xers were not looking to be lifelong sacrificial lambs for anyone, and had a low threshold for seeking alternative employment if their personal needs were not met.

Facing a clash of cultures in the workplace, Riccitiello realized that winning the hearts and minds of his people would require replacing "Do as I say," "Follow me," and "Do as I do" with a more people-friendly and engaging approach. In a 2014 Haas interview with Dean Richard Lyons, he said that this experience taught him that "people were inspired to pursue a vision they had a part in creating." In other words, bringing out the best in this particular audience required dialing up the democratic, coaching, and affiliative elements of his leadership style.

EXHIBIT #2: In response to a physician burnout rate that exceeded fifty percent, the Institute for Healthcare Improvement published a 2017 white paper that outlined a framework for improving joy in work. At the core of their model are "happy productive health people" and a participative management style in which leaders create space to hear, listen, and involve before acting. In this model, clear communication and consensus building are integral parts of the decision-making process.

Pioneers in this style of leadership within healthcare include Rich Isaacs, current CEO and Executive Director of The Permanente Medical Group and President and CEO of the Mid-Atlantic Medical Group. More than ten years prior to the release of the IHI white paper, while serving as the Physician-in-Chief at Kaiser South Sacramento, Rich established an expectation at his medical center that leaders regularly ask the people doing the work for their suggestions about what changes could be made to simultaneously improve their professional satisfaction and the quality of care they provided to their patients.

By giving everyone in the organization a voice, he created a culture of psychological safety and created unlimited opportunities for bottom-up engagement and positive change. Not surprisingly, under Rich's leadership, the South Sacramento medical center became a hotbed of innovations in care delivery, many of which were adopted as best practices throughout Northern California Kaiser.

EXHIBIT #3: One of my closest friends is Brad Crutchfield, a highly successful leader in the life sciences industry. Raised in San Diego, he was a high school superstar who excelled in the classroom and in athletics. He came to UC Davis with a plan to major in physiology and pre-med studies and possibly earn a spot on the roster of legendary coach Jim Sochor's championship football team. Things didn't quite work out for medical school or football, but he graduated on time and landed a nice job with Bio-Rad, a manufacturer of products for life science research and clinical diagnostics.

Brad assumed increasing levels of leadership responsibility at Bio-Rad and eventually became the President of their Life Sciences Group. One day, as we were enjoying some refreshing Corona beer on my back yard patio, I asked him for the secret to his leadership success. He said that he had a very simple technique that went like this: he met with his teams on a regularly scheduled basis and asked two questions: "What's working for you?" and "What's not working for you?" He took what was working and shared these best practices with other groups within the organization. More importantly, he worked to eliminate what wasn't working for his people so that they could be empowered to do their best work.

In my medical practice, I took care of many Bio-Rad employees who worked in various departments under Brad's direction. Curious how my poker buddy was perceived at work, I would ask them what they thought of Brad. Without exception, they sang his praises. Many volunteered that he was their best boss ever. When I asked why, they spoke of his frequent "What's working, what's not working?" meetings which made them feel heard, valued, and appreciated.

It should come as no surprise that Brad followed his tenure at Bio-Rad with other leadership positions at Illumina and QIAGEN and most recently took 10X Genomics public as its Chief Commercial Officer. While he did not play quarterback for the Aggies or become a doctor, I'd say he did quite well in life for himself and the companies and people he led by being a model servant leader.

CHAPTER 43

APPRECIATIVE INQUIRY

It makes me sad that human resources departments are often over-whelmed and consumed by issues related to the granddaddy of all-time sucks, disciplinary action. In a more perfect world, human resources specialists would have the bandwidth to focus on transformational work such as recruiting for fit, career counseling, leadership development, communications training, and intentionally creating the conversations, culture, and operations that maximize total performance.

Appreciative inquiry (Ai) can help that aspirational dream become a reality. The principles of Ai were established in the 1980s at Case Western Reserve University. David Cooperrider and Suresh Srivastva proposed that good things happen for a company and its people when team members are invited to focus on present positives rather than present problems. This deliberate spotlight on what's going right creates positive energy and inspires people to generate ideas for a better tomorrow that team members will be motivated to pursue without artificial incentives.

Juliette Tocino-Smith summarizes the principles of Ai in this way:

1. POSITIVE: positive questions enact positive change

2. CONSTRUCTIONIST: words create worlds

3. POETIC: life is expressed through story

4. SIMULTANEITY: inquiry creates change

5. ANTICIPATORY: imagination drives action

Mohr & Magruder Watkins's *"Roadmap for Creating Positive Futures"* outlines a five step rollout of Ai:

1. DEFINE: what is our desired outcome?

2. DISCOVERY: what are our strengths?

3. DREAM: what would work well in the future?

4. DESIGN: what do we need to do to make it happen?

5. DEPLOY: we're taking the action

Does Ai work? I can say from personal experience that it saved and transformed my former medical group into what it is today.

I had been with The Permanente Medical Group for six years when we hit the skids in 1995. In order to curb the skyrocketing cost of medical care, there was a national movement to reduce healthcare premiums by five percent per year for five consecutive years, and we bought into it along with most medical groups, hospitals, and insurance companies. This revenue death spiral had dire consequences. At one point we had only a few days of operating expenses in reserve.

Enter a new CEO, Dr. Robert Pearl, a Yale and Stanford-trained plastic surgeon who had previously served as the Physician-in-Chief of our Santa Clara Medical Center. Robbie was physically fit and tanned with dark brown hair combed neatly to the side. He typically wore a well-tailored dark blue suit, white shirt, and red tie, and completed his look with his signature brown boots. Even in a group of highly-educated and successful physicians, he stood out as exceptionally intelligent, confident, and focused.

Robbie took the helm of an ailing ship but did not focus on our problems. Instead, he spoke glowingly about our model of prepaid, integrated, evidence-based healthcare and the important role that physician leadership played in its success.

His first order of business was to host a series of dinner meetings with our colleagues throughout Northern California. At those meetings, he asked us what we wanted him to lead us to be. The two options he offered were to be the cost leader or to be the quality and service leader.

I remember a team of administrative assistants passing out pencils and paper ballots so that we could let him know our wishes. Of course the answer was a foregone conclusion. No one runs the gauntlet of medical school, residency, and fellowship training to spend a career as the cost leader. At every one of our medical centers, the vote was overwhelmingly that we wanted him to lead us to be the nation's quality and service leader. The difference between Robbie telling us what he was going to do and asking us what we wanted him to do was huge. To begin his tenure with an autocratic and authoritative leadership move would have been a non-starter during such challenging times. His decision to bring positive energy and hope to a dire situation and to ask for our input as his first order or business was a perfect implementation of the Ai method.

His marching orders now in hand, he was well positioned to use words and stories to paint the picture perfect postcard of our new corporate destination. This created a growth-mindset culture that empowered us to dream big dreams and make specific plans for how we would leverage our strengths to make iterative progress towards our ultimate goal, which was and is to be the model of healthcare for the nation.

Long story short, over several years Robbie transformed our medical group from a very good healthcare organization to a national leader in quality, service, patient satisfaction, and cost containment.

CHAPTER 44

DIVERSITY & INCLUSION

Ricky Winardi studied bioengineering at UC Berkeley and then worked with the US Department of Energy. This was followed by studying international health at Yale's School of Public Health, stints with UNICEF in New York City and the World Health Organization in Brazil, and medical school at the University of Connecticut.

I first met him when he was an internal medicine resident at the UC Davis Medical Center in Sacramento where I taught physicians-in-training once a week and recruited the best of them to join our medical group. Impressed by his rich and diverse background as well as his calm and humble demeanor, I offered him a job upon graduation.

Ricky joined our medical group and quickly fulfilled his promise and then some. Patients gravitated towards him because he was smart and really cared about people. After a few years, he joined the physician health and wellness committee that I chaired and brought to our work his passion for diversity and inclusion. We wanted to encourage his interests in these areas and sponsored him to attend an annual national diversity conference.

One year, soon after he returned from the conference, I asked him to share some highlights from his learnings. What Ricky told us has forever remained in my mind as the essential first step in meaningful diversity and inclusion work.

He said, *"Diversity is about finding common ground."* Before hearing those words, I had struggled with feelings of inadequacy about diversity because I was focused on all the things I did not know about people who were different from me.

The beauty of finding common ground as a first step in diversity work is that it invites everyone in the room to contribute their stories to an exploratory conversation about shared values. Invariably, the outcome is that people from divergent backgrounds find that they have many more similarities than differences, and those differences become objects of interest and further inquiry, rather than insurmountable barriers to collegiality and getting things done.

CHAPTER 45

INVERSION

The thought of a leader being solely responsible for a group's out-come conjures up an unsettling image of one person doing all the heavy lifting while a sea of humanity sits silently chewing gum and surf-ing social media. This is a common dilemma in education where the teacher is often held accountable for what should be a shared responsi-bility to learn.

Enter the concept of inversion where the students become the teach-ers and the teacher serves as a group facilitator. An example of this is the "flipped classroom" in which the majority of teacher-centered didactic instruction is done outside of the classroom via recorded video files. This frees up the in-person classroom time for group-oriented labs and prob-lem sets in which students take an active role in teaching one another.

Studies show that learning outcomes for the two models are roughly equivalent. But the real benefit of the flipped classroom is that students learn how to take ownership of their education and establish patterns for working collaboratively, as they will be asked to do in the work world.

Here's a humorous and powerful example of this theory in prac-tice. One of my patients was a long time substitute teacher at the high school level. I always wondered how subs could step into a calculus or US history class and effectively teach students. Were they themselves outstanding high school students with superb memories for content and concepts learned decades earlier?

My patient shared this substitute teaching secret that he swore never failed him: if a student asked a question that stumped him, he would pause, look up, and ask the class, "Is there anyone who has an idea about how to solve this problem?" He said that invariably, at least one student would volunteer an answer that either worked or seeded a productive conversation.

I applied a similar principle when I ran "code blues" in the hospital or emergency room on patients whose hearts or lungs had stopped working on their own. Of course, I would follow advanced life support protocols and call on my clinical experience. But at several steps along the way, especially if the patient was not responding favorably to chemicals or electric shocks, I would pause and ask other members of the team, "Does anyone have any other ideas about what to do next?"

One final example of the audience becoming the teacher comes from my work in physician health and wellness at our medical center. I co-chaired a monthly meeting of our wellness committee which was composed of busy clinicians. Already a big fan of inversion, it was my regular practice to solicit input from committee members. This generated a wide variety of ideas which ranged from cost-effective and easy to implement no brainers to elaborate, expensive and time-consuming projects.

One of the latter was my colleague Stacey Bowman's suggestion to host an annual family wellness retreat in Yosemite National Park. While that was a good idea, we were already sponsoring a long-standing similar event at Camp Sacramento in the Sierra mountains and it was very labor-intensive.

However, Stacey was not to be deterred. She was a pediatrician with a young family and believed in her heart of hearts that we needed to launch this additional event in Yosemite. I begrudgingly deferred to her enthusiasm, thinking that the best possible outcome would be her learning a painful lesson about the perils of event planning.

But Stacey proved me dead wrong.

She partnered with my talented committee co-chair, Diane Chan, and our world class administrative assistant, Tina Szura, to produce what has become one of our most popular annual events of all time. The Yosemite family weekend sells out every year within hours of being announced because Stacey knew that our colleagues and their families were yearning for this experience, and she put in the leadership work to make it happen.

Every year, attendees are treated to a combination of continuing medical education, family adventures in one of nature's most beautiful playgrounds, and a snazzy logo t-shirt designed by Stacey's husband, Steve.

The bottom line is that inversion works. One hundred one engaged people working as a team is much more productive than 1 person dragging 100 disengaged people in a direction they don't want to go.

CHAPTER 46

THE RIDER & THE ELEPHANT

*"Change happens in the boiler room of our emotions—
so find out how to light their fires."*

—*Jeff Dewar*

Jonathan Haidt, a social psychologist at New York University, uses the metaphor of the rider and the elephant to explain how human beings make decisions and change their behavior.

The rider is the analytical and rational part of our brain. We like to think that the rider is controlling our behavior. The elephant is the beastly emotional and irrational part of our brains. It is bigger and more power-ful than the rider and often rules the day. Thus the aphorisms "Emotion eats logic for lunch" and "Emotion bats last and bats a thousand."

Not convinced?

Think of the millions of people who make a decision to "get in shape." Following their riders' meticulous action plans, they buy lulu-lemon outfits, New Balance shoes, and Balega performance socks and pay for memberships to expensive fitness clubs. They work out five days a week for two weeks, two to three days a week for another month, and then quit. Why? It's such a hassle to pack and unpack gym clothes ev-ery day, they haven't lost any weight, and walking on the treadmill is so boring. In short order, workouts are replaced with extra large pepperoni pizzas, quarts of ice cream, and binging Korean dramas on Netflix.

The headline reads, "Elephants Crush Hapless Riders."

In order to change behavior and sustain new habits, the rider and elephant must work in harmony. The rider gets to set the goals, but the needy elephant must be made to feel good about the work, and the path to the promised land must be swept clear of obstacles.

Psychologist Sheri Pruitt's SMART change model covers all of these bases. Let's go back to our exercise example using her technique.

The **S** stands for: Set a goal. The rider needs to make it something manageable and understand the reason behind it. For example, if you are sedentary, set a goal to go to the gym twice a week for thirty minutes each time. Spend ten minutes walking on the treadmill, ten minutes on weights, and ten minutes stretching as you cool down. And know that the end game beyond any immediate exercise goal is improved health, wellness, and longevity.

M stands for: Monitor your progress. This can be as fancy as using a smartwatch to log your activity or as simple as checking a box on a piece of paper.

A stands for: Arrange your environment for success. If the elephant says it's a hassle to pack your gym bag in the morning, pack it the night before and put it in your trunk.

R stands for: Recruit a support team. Find someone who will hold you accountable for sticking with your program and achieving your goals. It's harder to let your fitness dream die if you have a cheerleader encouraging you to keep going when you fall short.

And finally, **T** stands for: Treat yourself along the way for achieving little and big goals. If you go to the club regularly for two weeks, treat yourself to a Spotify Premium subscription. When you achieve a big goal (such as crushing your Spin Class and receiving an invitation to be an instructor), book a nice weekend in San Francisco, complete with a visit to the zoo, where your inner elephant can hang out with his friends.

CHAPTER 47

A DYNAMIC DUO

My nephew Justin is a sophomore at Cal pursuing a degree in a relatively new and very popular major called Data Science.

From the UC Berkeley website: "The Data Science Major and Minor programs come in response to intensifying student, faculty, business, and societal demand amid the exponential growth of data in virtually all aspects of life. This transformation is generating a substantial unmet need for graduates who are not only technically proficient in analyzing data but who also know how to responsibly collect and manage data, and use data to make decisions and discoveries, think critically, and communicate effectively. The Data Science B.A., designed in collaboration with faculty from across the University, invests students with deep technical knowledge, expertise in how to apply that knowledge in a field of their choosing, and an understanding of the social and human contexts and ethical implications of how data are collected, analyzed and used. This combination positions graduates to help inform and develop solutions to a range of pressing challenges, from adapting industry to a new world of data, to amplifying learning in education, to helping communities recover from disaster."

Data scientists are in high demand because companies need them to find, clean, and organize data that helps them make better business decisions. But as the major description suggests, what the world needs most are analytics wonks who are rooted not only in their understanding of numbers (and the positive and negative implications of the use and misuse of data), but also in meaningful connections to people, society, and a moral compass that points to doing good.

Back to Justin. He is an Eagle Scout, and I see in him the qualities and character associated with those who have achieved that high honor. He is "trustworthy, loyal, helpful, friendly, courteous, kind, obedient, cheerful, thrifty, brave, clean, and reverent," personified.

I recently had the pleasure of sharing a cup of coffee and a nice conversation with him on Sproul Plaza, the storied public square on the south side of the Cal campus and the birthplace of the Free Speech Movement. When you sit with Justin, he's fully present in a calm and friendly way. He's not looking past you or checking his phone. He listens with great interest, asks good questions, and takes the conversation to deeper levels and interesting places. When he talks about himself, it's mostly about what he can do to help others and effect positive change in society.

I have no doubt that when he graduates, Justin will be hotly pursued by employers for his hard skills. But his employer will be getting much more than a data scientist. They will be hiring their next CEO.

CHAPTER 48

THE INTERSECTION OF D-I AND PI

Kelly and D-I

My daughter Kelly started her undergraduate studies at Cal Poly San Luis Obispo where she studied kinesiology and played on its nationally-ranked club lacrosse team.

After her sophomore year she transferred to UC Davis, switched her major to human development, and earned a roster spot on their Division 1 intercollegiate women's lacrosse team. She enjoyed the competition and level of play, though from my parental perspective, the experience looked like a brutal full-time job heaped on top of a heavy academic load.

Her D-I student-athlete life included early morning weight lifting, hours of practice, long road trips to snowy destinations, studying in airports and hotels, overcoming injuries, and navigating team and interpersonal relationships in an environment that placed a premium on winning games. What got Kelly through the season was a culture of family, teamwork, and mutual support among her teammates. This culture created a safe harbor for learning important life lessons while riding the tumultuous waves of a long season and fostered deep relationships that have continued to grow stronger beyond college.

Upon graduation Kelly took a job in Human Resources with LinkedIn at their worldwide headquarters in the Silicon Valley. Think huge campus spanning several blocks, free gourmet food, on site gymnasiums, and numerous other perks that keep employees happy.

Her new hire cohort of three included two women who brought with them several years of work experience in Human Resources. At the end of the first day of orientation, her supervisor sat down with the three new hires and said, "Let's talk about teamwork. What's teamwork?"

From a professional perspective, Kelly was the least qualified to answer the question. But moved by youthful enthusiasm and drawing on her years of experience in competitive sports, she blurted out, "Teamwork is about everyone being on the same page, everyone on the team making a contribution, and the team getting better every day."

Rob and PI

My friend and colleague Rob Mclaughlin was raised in the Central Valley town of Stockton, California, and like my daughter Kelly, earned his undergraduate degree at UC Davis. Following medical school at UC San Francisco, residency at the University of Pennsylvania, and fellowship training at Stanford, he joined our medical group as a head and neck surgeon with a subspecialty in facial plastic and reconstructive surgery.

He took on multiple leadership roles including oversight for our process improvement (PI) initiatives. A quick study, he became a deep well of information about the fundamentals and nuances of the PDSA (Plan-Do-Study-Act) cycle that lie at the core of evolving from good to great. He approached me about partnering with him to prepare the curriculum for a two hour workshop on PI that would be rolled out to all physicians at our medical center. While I did not have a background in this work, I was experienced in public speaking and group facilitation so we made a good team.

Rob sent me his preliminary PowerPoint presentation and it included 189 information-dense slides that read like a CliffsNotes version of *War and Peace*. It was a *tour de force* but Rob and I worried that it ran the risk of overwhelming our audience to the point of disengagement. We pared down the slides from 189 to 75 and took a step back to figure out how we could lump the remaining content into a handful of categories that would give our audience a framework for the important information we were presenting.

At which point I had an "aha" moment and realized that all of our content about process improvement fell into one of the three categories that Kelly used to define teamwork: everyone needed to be on the same page about our medical group's purpose and mission; everyone on the team needed to contribute to the work if we are to be successful; and the ultimate goal of our process improvement work was to get better as a team every day. We tagged each slide with a colorful tab that read "ALIGN" "ENABLE," or "IMPROVE" and it helped our audience to more easily digest and absorb our PI message.

CHAPTER 49

THE ELEVATOR PITCH

An elevator pitch is a brief and powerful story intended to sell an idea, product, or organization. As its name implies, it should take no longer than a short elevator ride to deliver it. Done well, an elevator pitch moves its audience to take action.

Masterfully delivering an elevator pitch is an important skill for anyone who wants to get things done. Whether managing up or down, telling a persuasive story that appeals to your audience's rider and elephant increases the odds that they will buy what you are selling.

This style of impactful storytelling does not come naturally to most people. Fortunately, coaches like Dick Butterfield can make learning this skill engaging and fun. While an undergraduate at Stanford, Dick developed leadership and public speaking skills through his work in student government. He further honed his oratorical repertoire while earning his MFA at the A.C.T. Conservatory in San Francisco, where he subsequently served as the Dean and a member of the acting and voice faculty.

Butterfield calls elevator pitches *powerbites* and advises the following recipe:

1. Start with your conclusion: "Serotonin Surge Charities restores hope and healing for the most vulnerable members of our communities."

2. Give three pieces of evidence for your conclusion: "Ten percent of our local population does not have medical insurance to cover the cost of their medical care"; "We are a grass
roots nonprofit organization that leverages volunteerism and
collaboration to financially support safety net medical clinics that care for these uninsured neighbors"; "Over the past
twenty years, we have raised over $4 million to support these
clinics that provide 250,000 patient care visits per year to individuals and families who would otherwise go without care."

3. Call to action (the answer to the audience's question, "Why
should I care?"): "If you share our vision of a more perfect
world in which everyone has access to medical care, please
join our team and make that dream a reality for all members
of our community.

Of course, powerbites are just the tip of the iceberg in communication. Through his company *Butterfield Speaks*, Dick and his associates
help high-profile clients from Microsoft, LinkedIn, Google, and Kaiser
Permanente deliver clear, persuasive messages and work more effectively with the media. His *Power of Persuasion* curriculum features three
areas of communication excellence: accessing your power to persuade;
discovering and developing your message; and mastering your craft as
a communicator.

My favorite Dick Butterfield teaching module is titled "From
Monotone to Magical." He uses his rich baritone voice, Shakespear-
ean acting skills, and entertaining sense of humor to demonstrate how
modulating the volume and cadence of your speech, waking up your
facial muscles, and clearly articulating your words transforms a lifeless
narrative into a compelling story that leaves your audience calling for
an encore performance.

CHAPTER 50

Non-Negotiables & Guardrails

I n their 2014 book, *Scaling Up Excellence: Getting to More Without Settling for Less*, Bob Sutton and Huggy Rao use a religious analogy to describe the spectrum of leadership styles and the effects they have on an organization's people and success.

At one extreme lies Catholicism, a top-down, one-way, air attack that results in early landmark achievements but soon thereafter leads to disregard and disengagement. At the opposite end of the spectrum sits Buddhism, a bottom up, mashup, ground war that produces local autonomy and individual joy but suffers from widespread inconsistency. Images of the Vietnam War with the United States' aerial bombing campaign versus the Viet Cong's boots on the ground approach come to mind. They review case studies that point out the pros and cons of these two leadership styles, and describe the circumstances that would make them good or bad fits for the task at hand.

Sutton and Rao describe a third leadership style that lies between Catholicism and Buddhism. This middle ground alternative begins with defining the organization's non-negotiable core competencies and deliverables. For The Permanente Medical Group, those would include operational excellence, an exceptional care experience, and joy and meaning for the people providing the care.

The next step is to establish guardrails for organizational conversations, culture, and operations that keep people thinking and acting in a defined arena that empowers the company and its people to deliver on its core promises. If you have ever bowled with the bumpers up, you will understand how setting such guardrails can improve performance by eliminating the dreaded gutter balls and keeping more balls in play to produce the strikes and spares that lead teams to victory.

CHAPTER 51

THE ESSENTIAL ROLE OF REST

The book of *Exodus* tells the story of God delivering to Moses the Ten Commandments, a set of rules related to ethics and worship. The fourth commandment is "To remember the Sabbath Day, to keep it holy." This commandment was a nod to God's creation week story and the special status he had conferred on the seventh day as one of rest. If God almighty needed to rest after heavy lifting, how could we not?

This principle of allowing a period of rest and recovery after doing hard work is also sacrosanct to high performance athletes. In their quest to be the best, they push their bodies past the usual limits, often causing acute or chronic damage to their musculoskeletal system.

Days off from training are required to allow their bodies to repair, rebuild, and strengthen. Failure to interrupt activity with rest can result in major damage, a common example being a baseball pitcher shredding a rotator cuff tendon due to insufficient rest between starts.

While few of us are high performance athletes, most of us are at risk for self-harm due to overly scheduled lives that leave little room for physical, emotional, and spiritual rest and recovery. We face an unrelenting onslaught of what I call Multiple Simultaneous Conflicting Imperatives, and the acronym MSCI is appropriately pronounced "messy".

Does this schedule boiling over with MSCI sound familiar? You wake up tired (pick a reason: sleep apnea, chronic back pain, a relationship gone sour that left you going to sleep angry, a neighbor blasting

Led Zeppelin at 3 a.m.); you go to the bathroom and you notice blood in your stool and on the toilet paper (but there was a burning and tearing sensation as you passed your stool, so hopefully the blood is due to a hemorrhoid rather than the colon cancer your sister had); you go to the kitchen for some breakfast and there's no milk for your cereal; your kids need you to make their breakfast and lunch.

You are late for work which isn't good because you are already on probation; your manager makes unwanted sexual advances but you can't speak up because you are the only wage earner in your family, you are already buried in credit card debt, and you can't afford to lose this job; after you go out of your way to help an especially needy client, he files a formal complaint and accuses you of being aloof and uncaring; you get a call during an important lunch meeting that your son has been sent home with head lice; a computer meltdown at work prevents you from accessing your spreadsheets for hours so you stay at the office until 7:30 p.m. to get the job done—which means that you've missed yet another one of your daughter's soccer games.

You go home hoping for a nice quiet family dinner but find your kids eating frozen dinners because your spouse is out for another night of poker; said spouse comes home a little tipsy and brimming with an eagerness to talk about the state of your relationship; you have no desire to talk about relationships because you are exhausted and hangry (hungry and angry).

You put on some tennis shoes and head out to walk the dog and claim some wellness for yourself; when you walk fast you get chest pain, shortness of breath, and nausea—just like your father did before he had a quadruple bypass surgery.

And did I mention that the mail is piling up (and it's important stuff like automobile recalls, unpaid bills, and a fat letter from the IRS); your mother was in the emergency room again with another near fainting episode that her doctor can't figure out; there's a greasy puddle of liquid in your driveway where your car was parked; and your dog's anal glands need to be decompressed before they rupture on your living room couch. It's enough to drive you insane.

One way to interrupt this madness is to schedule rest time into your calendar. The absence of activity allows wiggle room for scheduled events to run over and creates blank slate opportunities to be spontaneous and respond (or not) to whatever comes your way.

Another creative option for rest is described in the 1990 book *Healthy Pleasures*. Psychologist Robert Ornstein and physician David Sobel ask us to "Imagine a world without pleasure. Life would appear colorless and humorless. A baby's smile would go unappreciated. Foods would be tasteless. The beauty of a Bach concerto would fall on deaf ears. Feelings like joy, thrills, delights, ecstasy, elation and happiness would disappear. The company of others would not bring comfort and joy."

They remind us that pleasure can be nurtured through the senses and positive emotions. They encourage us to frequently treat ourselves to known pleasurable activities such as eating popcorn at a matinee movie, cuddling with a puppy, and reading a good book. We should also have fun searching for new healthy pleasures that will help us to comfortably remain in the land of the living.

CHAPTER 5 2

LIVE OUTSIDE THE BOX, AND GET SASSY WHEN NECESSARY

Do you know high energy, creative people who bring fresh perspectives and new ideas to old problems? Such people are fun to be around, and challenge us to reconsider outdated ways of thinking that leave us mired in stale habits and inaction.

My friend Tracy Kaplan doesn't just think outside the box, she lives there. She graduated from Berkeley Law and earned her master's level executive coaching certification from Columbia University. As the owner and managing principal of a consulting company, she helps leaders clarify their core values, intentions, and vision for the future. Her energy, crisp thinking, and clear communication help people get from Point A to Point B.

I got a glimpse of her creative thought process and *joie de vivre* while our families were eating out together at The Graduate, a sports bar and restaurant located across the street from the campus of UC Davis.

The Grad enjoyed a storied fifty-year run before closing its doors to business in 2019. When you walked into The Grad, you headed to the register on the left to place your order and then found a seat at one of the central picnic tables or perimeter booths. Either way, you were treated to a celebratory and comfortable vibe created by multiple giant screens, fans cheering for their teams, pitchers of beer, and the smell of burgers and fries.

When we sat down, I asked Tracy what she had ordered for lunch. She replied, "A veggie burger, add bacon." Davis is a liberal university town filled with vegans and vegetarians, so I totally understood the request for a veggie burger. And lots of native Davisites enjoy their meat, especially those who grew up ranching, hunting, and fishing in what feels like a slice of the Midwest plopped down in Northern California. But I had never seen or heard of anyone ordering bacon on a veggie burger.

Tracy explained her choice like this. She likes the taste and health benefits of a veggie patty, but she also loves bacon (no explanation necessary). And she thinks the two go really well together. When you think about it, that makes total sense. Just because you like plant based products doesn't mean you don't like meat. And you can't assume that people who crave bacon don't also harbor a great appreciation and appetite for food that grows in the ground.

My friend Lisa brings a big bolus of energy to everything she touches, and she definitely knows how to sprinkle a dash of sass and humor on whatever she's serving up.

We were once noodling about how we could convince a colleague to make an important decision that we both saw as favorable. After following a course of action that covered all of the traditional bases, we found ourselves at an impasse.

One day, she sent me a message saying that she had closed the deal with "a hundy, a forty, and a pair of fishnet stockings." Yikes. Had she compromised her values and broken rules to get us over the final hurdle? To my great sense of relief, she later elaborated that her comment was a humorous metaphor for turning on the charm, not a detailed account of bribery and debauchery.

The take home lessons from Tracy and Lisa are that getting things done often requires thinking in new and creative ways, and that sometimes, even the most substantial of pitches requires some sass and Sriracha hot sauce to push it over the top and across the finish line.

CHAPTER 53

SALMAGUNDI

Just a few additional thoughts that I've thrown together to close out this section on getting things done.

The first is that you need to focus on achieving a task that is possible. Not to say that you can't do big things, but to quote David Allen, "You can do anything, but not everything."

So for example, through good planning and execution, Kaiser Permanente can be the model for healthcare in America, but not by haphazardly doing everything for everyone however and whenever they want it. That would not be smart, evidence-based medicine and it would burn out the organization's people in a matter of weeks.

The second I learned from Brad Brewer, a protege of Arnold Palmer and professional golf coach. I attended one of his four-hour seminars as part of a medical conference in Orlando, Florida. The idea was that some principles of golf had practical applications in the improvement of medical care. Made sense to me, and hanging out on a driving range and putting green sure beat sitting in a lecture hall.

During a tutorial on lag putting, a type of long putt intended to get you close to the hole, but not necessarily in it, Mr. Brewer advised that the speed and distance of the putt were just as important as the direction. This was news to me, and most other high handicappers, who spend more time thinking about where to aim a putt than how hard to strike the ball.

The latter turns out to be more important because if you miss the putt (which is highly likely on a long putt), it determines whether the ball ends up close enough to the hole to be easily holed on the next putt.

The practical application for the work world is that achieving goals requires not only your team setting out in the right direction, but also putting in the right amount of time and effort to make it to your destination. Much like a rocket launch into space, not enough thrust will never get you into orbit, and too much thrust will send you into the vast abyss.

The third is a repeat of my comments about keeping a calendar and to-do list in the earlier Work World section. This is one of a precious few pearls that I have chosen to repeat because it is easy to implement and will result in immediate returns. Plus behavioral scientists claim that you have to hear something between 10–20 times before taking action on it.

The fourth is something I've learned in my older age: with a short horizon comes clarity. Unlike a twenty-year-old who can find comfort and a convenient excuse in saying, "I'll figure it out when I'm older," being sixty IS the older that young people speak of. So with regards to asking and answering life's big questions and getting things done before you die, it's a matter of now or never.

PART V

STRUGGLES

CHAPTER 54

OUR PREDICAMENT

One of the best things about my career has been the privilege of listening to my patients' stories. Unlike the superficial conversations we share in polite social situations, patient stories in the doctor's office occur behind closed doors in a place of psychological safety.

They are full octane, unfiltered, and comprised of two things: complaints about signs (things that can be seen or measured such as a fever or rash) and symptoms (sensations that the patient can feel but that others cannot see or measure, such as pain and fatigue); and more importantly, concerns about the causes and consequences of their signs and symptoms.

After listening to a few hundred thousand of these stories over three decades, I have yet to meet a person who does not have a tale of woe lurking below their thin veneer of wellness. As Brene Brown says, "Everybody has a story that will break your heart. And if you are really paying attention, most people have a story that will bring you to your knees." The particulars of our distress are diverse, but the end result is always the same: we feel unsettled at best, despondent at worst, and we are separated from our joy and meaning.

This observation leads me to conclude that our primary predicament as human beings is how to live a good life while navigating an unavoidable and daunting gauntlet of pain, isolation, shame, suffering, disability, and ultimately death. Haven't experienced any of these things yet? Just wait, they are coming.

CHAPTER 55

ITS RESOLUTION

Just as our suffering is universal, so is our hope. In 1992, John Gard-
ner submitted an essay to the *Western Journal of Medicine* titled
"Personal Renewal" in which he offered this uplifting perspective: "For
many this life is a vale of tears; for no one is it free of pain. But we are
so designed that we can cope with it if we can live within some context
of meaning. Given that powerful help, we can draw on the deep springs
of the human spirit, to see our suffering in the framework of all human
suffering, to accept the gifts of life with thanks and endure life's indignities with dignity."

Following a review of the literature, extensive work with burned-
out healthcare professionals, and over three decades of learning about
the breadth and depth of the human experience through my patients,
I've come to the conclusion that the resolution of our predicament and
the attainment of joy and meaning lie in the adoption and consistent
practice of four life-changing habits: mindfulness, gratitude, cultivating
relationships, and positive adaptation.

CHAPTER 56

MINDFULNESS

*"If you board the wrong train, it is no use
running along the corridor in the opposite direction."*

—Dietrich Bonhoeffer

The present moment, with all of its annoyances and crises, more than deserves our full attention and decision-making capabilities. However, most of us live in a world of distraction and multitasking, frustrated by our inability to focus on the issues at hand and get things done in an orderly fashion.

The solution to this chaos is mindfulness, Jon Kabat-Zinn's secular pullout of Buddhist contemplative practices. It is an awareness that arises from intentionally paying attention to the present moment, free from judgement, and undistracted by regrets about the past and anxiety about the future. It works like this: the next time you are faced with a stressor and its associated tension, take a slow deep breath and remind yourself that you have a choice about how you will respond to the tension. As you exhale, let go of those long-standing maladaptive responses and choices that no longer serve you well. Examples might include negative judgements, social withdrawal, and avoidance behaviors such as drinking and gambling.

Take the time you need to mindfully choose responses that lead to wellness. Options include self-compassion, positive distractions, exercise, and prayer. Such choices have the power to favorably reset the trajectory of your life journey. In the words of William Jennings Bryan, "Destiny is not a matter of chance. It is a matter of choice. It is not a thing to be waited for. It is a thing to be achieved."

Bottom line: slow down, be mindful, and make good choices.

CHAPTER 57

GRATITUDE

"Gratitude is not only the greatest of virtues,
but the parent of all the others."

—*Cicero*

When I was about ten years old my father, a minister who called on numerous sick people in the hospital, advised me that I should be grateful every morning I could wake up and pee. You can imagine how this comment made little sense to me as a fifth grader who was peeing just fine.

It wasn't until 10 years later, while studying anatomy and physiology, that I began to understand what my father meant—namely that we should never take for granted the miraculous ways that the human body works because soon enough those highly evolved functions like swallowing, peeing, speaking, and thinking will begin to falter—sometimes in the split second it takes to be struck down by a falling tree branch or stroke.

Gratitude is a thankful appreciation for what you have already received. The research of Bob Emmons has shown that people who are grateful enjoy superior physical, emotional, and social health. A simple way to be more grateful is to keep a gratitude journal and start each day by writing down three things you are grateful for.

Along the same lines, instead of waking up every day and saying to yourself, "Woe is me," proclaim "WOW is me!" WOW that you woke up instead of dying in your sleep; WOW that you stayed dry overnight and can empty your bladder and bowel on your own terms; and WOW that for one more day you have meaningful work and the strength to do it.

When challenged to declare the one best thing about gratitude, Emmons replies, "freedom." Freedom from circumstances dictating our moods, freedom from always having to clamor for credit, and freedom to acknowledge the accomplishments of others.

CHAPTER 58

CULTIVATING RELATIONSHIPS

*"Close relationships are the coin of the realm
in the Kingdom of Wellness."*

—Me

As stated earlier in the opening section of this book, family physician and author Richard Swenson contends that the connections forged in our social, emotional, and spiritual lives are the primary drivers of our wellness.

Social Life—The hierarchy of social relationships spans from loneliness, to connection, to connection for the greater good. In a 2019 Scientific American essay titled "Loneliness Is Harmful to Our Nation's Health," Lasker Foundation President Dr. Claire Pomeroy points out that 47% of Americans often feel alone and disconnected from meaningful relationships. This loneliness has numerous negative emotional and physical consequences, including high blood pressure, heart disease, diabetes, obesity, dementia, depression, and suicide. Conversely, as demonstrated in Harvard's 75-year study of adult development, connecting with others through deep and long-lasting relationships is the primary driver of human health and happiness, far outweighing factors such as status, income, and residential zip codes. In *Me to We: Finding Meaning in a Material World,* Craig and Marc Kielburger define the ultimate relationship, the type that maximizes joy and meaning, as one in which individuals commit to working together for a cause greater than themselves.

Emotional Life—Your relationship with thoughts and feelings and the story you tell yourself about you is called your emotional life. It's normal to have the occasional blues and to harbor self-doubt, but many of us live with a pervasive negative narrative. The British rock band Keane captures this phenomenon in "The Way I Feel": "There's something wrong about the way I feel, a missing link, a broken part, a punctured wheel."

An essential first step in establishing a healthy emotional life is to take inventory of your values and to compose a personal mission statement based on those values. Only then can you pursue a values-congruent life, one in which you choose thoughts and actions that help you live on purpose.

As you consider what you truly believe in and what you are trying to get done in your one life, I refer you once again to David Brooks' 2015 opinion article, "The Moral Bucket List," in which he challenges us to take a look at the relative merits of pursuing resume virtues (think prestigious university degree, fancy awards, and material wealth) and eulogy virtues (the ones talked about at your funeral; were you kind, brave, honest, faithful, and capable of deep love?).

Cultivating a healthy emotional life is hard work, but the benefits are innumerable. If you need some help, I recommend working with a counselor or coach.

Spiritual Life—A 2010 survey showed that worldwide, 43% of people believe in God or a supreme being. The range of belief spanned from 4% in Japan, to 70% in the United States, to 93% in Indonesia. A more recent Pew Foundation report suggests a downward trend in America, with the percentage of respondents being absolutely certain that God exists dropping from 71% to 63% from 2007 to 2014.

This can be partially explained by Darwin's 1859 *The Origin of Species*, Mendel's unraveling of the mystery behind smooth and wrinkled peas, and the Manhattan Project's creation of the atomic bomb. Such discoveries and inventions have led some to conclude that human beings are the ultimate source of knowledge, wisdom, and power and that a belief in God is irrational.

Suffice it to say that others believe Mendel is Mendel and God is God and that a belief in God is not *irrational*, but rather *transrational*, or beyond human reasoning. For these people, their relationship with God and decision to serve God is the primary driver of their joy and meaning.

For others, the doubt is not about a loving God but rather formal religion's crimes against humanity (think the Crusades and priest pedophilia). Such actions are indefensible, and a loving God is surely disappointed by such bad choices and behavior (but certainly not surprised, human nature being what it is).

The newspaper columnist Abigail Van Buren (of "Dear Abby" fame) weighs in on despicable behavior by religious organizations and their people by reminding us that "the church is a hospital for sinners, not a museum for saints."

For the sake of perspective, it is also important to recognize the generations of religious organizations, leaders, and people who have faithfully lived out their promises to love God, love people, and leave this world a better place than they found it.

CHAPTER 59

POSITIVE ADAPTATION

We seek the comfort of stability and sameness, but Heraclitus' proclamation that "the only constant in life is change" rules the day.

Some changes are easily overcome, but others such as the loss of a job, dissolution of a marriage and family, or death of a child are devastating and send victims free falling into a deep and dark crevasse where they come face-to-face with the five stages of grief described by Elisabeth Kubler-Ross: denial, anger, bargaining, depression, and acceptance.

Effectively adapting to such turmoil is an essential skill of a life well-lived. In his book *Switch: How to Change Things When Change is Hard*, Chip Health reminds us that in the wake of change and challenges, there are always individuals and groups who are adapting more favorably than others. He calls these super adaptors "bright spots" and advises that the most effective way for us to deal with change is to either be a bright spot or learn from bright spots.

My personal version of this practice is to maintain a "liger" (from the movie *Napoleon Dynamite*, "It's pretty much my favorite animal. It's like a lion and a tiger mixed, bred for its skills in magic") composed of my favorite role models for positive adaptation. When faced with high stakes stressors, I bring forth my best effort by imitating the habits that these people have used to overcome adversity.

Adopting a positive mindset is another powerful tool for maintaining joy and meaning when swimming in a pond of pain. Remarkable examples of the power of mindset were the 29% of women Holocaust survivors, who when interviewed as older adults, said they had lived a good life. How could this be? Sociologist Aaron Antonovsky found that these women had an unflappable sense of coherence—a deeply held belief that despite circumstances that screamed otherwise, life was comprehensible, manageable, and meaningful.

And while it is true that no sane person would invite tragedy into their life, cataclysmic change is often the catalyst for positive transformation. Based on her work with terminally ill patients, Kubler-Ross observed that suffering can fill its hosts with newfound empathy, compassion, and a deep loving concern for others. Adds Mark Thibodeaux in *God's Voice Within*, ". . . dark times can be breakthrough moments in our own salvation history," creating opportunities for repentance, fortitude, humility, patience, trust, self-assurance, self-confidence, and wisdom.

This principle of goodness emerging from our brokenness finds its artistic home in kintsugi, the Japanese practice of repairing broken pottery by filling its fracture lines with gold. The resulting masterpiece is a moving metaphor for our capacity to adapt to suffering and emerge as more beautiful people.

Finally, suffering, experienced firsthand or vicariously through the life of another, also gives us a realistic perspective of how full or empty our glass is compared to others, and whether it is filled with wine or urine.

Case in point: early in my medical career, I worked with Larry, an upbeat licensed vocational nurse who sported a flat top hairdo and wore a striped Ben Davis work shirt to cover his big belly. Larry had previously seen duty as a helicopter medic in Vietnam where it was his team's job to swoop down into the jungle to scoop up the victims of war, some of them dead, many so badly injured that they wished they were dead.

In the wake of a challenging patient interaction that left me feeling angry and defeated, I found myself venting to Larry about the difficulty of my job. After listening to my story with compassion, he offered this gem of advice based on his harrowing wartime experience: "Young man, if you have a job that only has two bad days a week, you've got a great job."

To this day, I rejoice every week I experience two or less bad days.

CHAPTER 60

Feed the Right Inner Wolf

*"Our brains are like Velcro for negative experiences,
but Teflon for positive ones."*

—*Rick Hanson, PhD, UC
Berkeley's Greater Good Science Center*

Over millions of years, our brains have evolved to have a built-in negativity bias. That is to say, we tend to notice and hang onto the bad and disregard or let go of the good. This is considered to be an evolutionary advantage because remembering where the wild man-eating beasts lay in wait is a matter of life and death, whereas retaining the image of a beautiful sunrise is merely pleasurable.

The main problems with allowing the negativity bias to rule our modern-day lives are that 1) we've done an excellent job of curbing the population of free-roaming man-eating beasts, so living in fear of being eaten alive is unnecessary; 2) it fosters a "Debbie Downer" mentality that paints an overly dark picture of all that is good and bad in our lives.

Indeed, you may have experienced a day that featured waking up refreshed, a hot cup of morning coffee a paired with a delicious pineapple coconut scone, time for a brisk walk during your lunch hour, positive kudos from your boss for work well done, and your favorite sports team beating its archrival. Yet for most of that day, you were consumed by anger over a newspaper editorial inconsistent with your political views and resentment about not being invited to Roland's birthday party.

The good news, according to Dr. Hanson and others who study neuro-plasticity, the science of rewiring your brain, is that you can level the playing field by tilting toward that which is positive.

Dr. Barbara Fredrickson, a professor of psychology and neuroscience at the University of North Carolina, is a pioneer in this arena of positive psychology. In the late 1990's, she developed a broaden-and-build the-ory of positive emotions which postulated that positive emotions such as joy, interest, contentment, and love fostered a heightened awareness of that which was good, and also inspired the long-term development and accumulation of adaptive thoughts and behaviors that contributed to one's resilience, health, and well-being. This steady upward spiral of positive emotions and positive adaptation offers an appealing alternative to a life focused on negative stimuli that trigger a chaotic cacophony of short-term survival-oriented solutions.

This principle is found in "The Two Wolves," a parable about the importance of choosing the right attitudes that is often attributed to the Cherokee people. The Chief discloses to his grandson that a battle between two wolves lives within him. One wolf is good and lives in harmony with everyone. He is filled with joy, humility, and kindness. The other wolf is filled with anger, envy, regret, greed, and self-pity and fights with everyone for no reason. Both wolves are fighting to win the Chief's spirit.

The grandson asks which wolf will survive. The Chief replies, "The one I feed."

CHAPTER 61

THE REAL BAD ASSES

In 1910, Teddy Roosevelt delivered a lengthy speech titled "Citizen in a Republic" at La Sorbonne in Paris. Embedded in that speech was a powerful passage that endures over one hundred years later as a source of encouragement for those who dare greatly in life. It is also a stinging rebuke of those who sit in the peanut gallery, afraid to take risks themselves, yet eager to criticize those who do.

The passage is called "The Man in the Arena" and reads, "It is not the critic who counts; not the man who points out how the strong man stumbles, or where the doer of deeds could have done them better. The credit belongs to the man who is actually in the arena, whose face is marred by dust and sweat and blood; who strives valiantly; who errs, who comes up short again and again, because there is no effort without error and shortcoming; but who does actually strive to do the deeds; who knows great enthusiasms, the great devotions; who spends himself in a worthy cause; who at the best knows in the end the triumph of high achievement, and who at the worst, if he fails, at least fails while daring greatly, so that his place shall never be with those cold and timid souls who neither know neither victory nor defeat."

You can see why champion of the arena Nelson Mandela drew inspiration from these words and why midshipmen at the US Naval Academy are required to commit the passage to memory.

Brene Brown, a University of Houston sociology professor and expert on courage, vulnerability, shame, and empathy, offers us an updated version of the man in the arena. She describes a champion who dares greatly and tells the truth about her experience. In her 2012 book *Rising Strong: How the Ability to Reset Transforms the Way We Live, Love, Parent, and Lead*, she writes, "People who wade into discomfort and vulnerability and tell the truth about their stories are the real badasses."

> *"What's the difference between God and a surgeon?*
> *God doesn't think He's a surgeon."*
> —Source unknown

Taylor Riall, a professor of surgery at the University of Arizona, is an example of the modern day badass. Following medical school, residency, and a pancreatobiliary fellowship at Johns Hopkins, the mecca of American surgical training, she earned a Ph.D. at the University of Texas Medical Branch in Galveston. She is currently the Interim Chair of the Department of Surgery at the University of Arizona, where she performs complex surgeries on patients with advanced cancer.

In 2018, while serving as the President of the Society of University Surgeons, she delivered a speech at the Academic Surgical Congress titled, "Enjoy the Journey." In it, she disclosed her story of personal burnout and emphasized the important roles that mindfulness, self-awareness, and emotional intelligence played in her recovery and resilience.

Her audience numbered in the hundreds and included her mentors, colleagues, and surgeons-in-training from America's leading academic medical centers. While diverse in gender, age, and their unique pathways into medicine, what they all shared was their immersion in a deep-rooted surgical culture infamous for its arrogance, abusive behavior, and intolerance of perceived weaknesses.

Dr. Riall's courageous personal disclosure served many purposes: it validated that issues of burnout were real for surgeons, including one of

its most highly-decorated and respected superstars; it jump-started positive changes in the conversations, culture, and operations that determine
the wellness (and unwellness) or surgeons worldwide; it planted the seed
for a climate of psychological safety in which surgeons can express their
challenges and still be affirmed as colleagues worthy of respect and trust;
and it saved the lives and careers of those in her audience who felt like
they were the only ones suffering with feelings of inadequacy, despair,
and shame.

> *"People make mistakes, that's why they put rubbers*
> *on the ends of erasers."*
> —*Fleabag*

Self-compassion and self-forgiveness for past mistakes and trans-
gressions is another important habit of the badass. The "armor up and be
perfect" *modus operandi* commonly found in high achievers casts them
in roles where they are asked to tackle the world's most daunting and
complex problems. However, perfection is seldom possible when problem managing global climate change, overpopulation, and pandemics, or
dealing with the ugly underbelly of human behavior.

For people who ascribe to the *Anna Karenina* principle and only see
success in that which is perfect, such enigmas are sources of frustration
and feelings of failure. Wayne Sotile, a pioneer in resilience counseling
for healthcare professionals, reminds us that the "superperson syndrome"
perpetuated by high stakes training programs invariably leads to guilt,
shame, and humiliation.

> *"If shot by an arrow, your job is*
> *to not shoot yourself with more arrows."*
> —*Jon Kabat-Zinn*

Brene Brown offers a solution to this dilemma and calls it whole-heart-
ed living. It begins with a position of self-worth. Wake up each morning

thinking "My best efforts today will be enough." Spend eight to four-teen hours swimming in the sea of victories, defeats, and indignities that make up the typical day. Then go to bed believing, "Yes, I am imperfect and vulnerable and sometimes afraid, but that doesn't change the truth that I am also brave and worthy of love and belonging." Get a good night's sleep and repeat.

I have taken Dr. Brown's words to heart by adopting the imperfect but sturdy cockroach as my spirit animal.

For the first eight years of my life, I came to admire these insects while living with my family in a two-bedroom flat at 1134 Jackson Street in San Francisco's Nob Hill neighborhood, a few uphill blocks west of Chinatown. Not knowing that these critters were regarded as filthy pests, I remember proudly packing one up in an empty jelly jar to bring to my first kindergarten show-and-tell. Vicky Jew's spindly spider looked so weak compared to my dark brown, armor-clad gladiator.

It's not that I don't appreciate the majesty of a bald eagle as it soars in the sky looking for prey or don't acknowledge the majestic lion as the king of the jungle. It's just that I have developed a deep-rooted respect for the cockroach nation's unequaled survival skills and ability to with-stand everything that the human race throws at it, from cans of Raid to the potent poisons and traps laid by pest exterminator professionals.

Granted, cockroaches are commoners, and no one cockroach stands out as student body president material, but you don't see many of them mired in self-pity and getting down on themselves. And as we all know from personal experience, while you may be able to successfully keep cockroaches at bay for a while, in the end, they will return, with friends.

"The man who opts for revenge should dig two graves."
—*Chinese proverb*

Once you get comfortable forgiving yourself for being less than per-fect, try forgiving others too. Pick the person who has bothered you the absolute most and who keeps you up at night with thoughts of your moral superiority and their painful and slow death. This person either committed a major transgression against you, or killed you slowly with a thousand paper cuts over many years.

Either way, please know that while you are losing sleep and years of life perseverating on their evilness and how undeserving they are of life, they are not thinking about you at all. In fact, it is fairly likely that they have a personality disorder that pushes your buttons and allows them to live contentedly with a total disregard for you and your feelings. So just let it go!

Don't believe me?

Then consider this admonition from Nelson Mandela, a man who had many reasons to be filled with resentment but found better ways to spend his precious time: "Resentment is like drinking poison and hoping that your enemies will die." In other words, in the end, resentment only hurts the person who harbors it.

CHAPTER 62

LESSONS FROM A JET FIGHTER PILOT

When the COVID-19 pandemic hit, healthcare professionals went on high alert and gathered ranks to do battle against an unfamiliar and dangerous enemy that was quickly infiltrating all parts of the world and leaving death and disability in its destructive path.

As a physician health and wellness leader, I asked myself who I could turn to for helpful advice that could provide some guidance and reassurance about how to approach and conquer this medical version of all-out war. The answer was a family friend who serves in the US armed forces as a jet fighter pilot. He's the real deal All-American. A smart, athletic, and focused young man who got it in his mind at an early age that he wanted to serve his country by flying an airplane really fast. In *Divergent*, Veronica Roth writes, "Fear doesn't shut you down, it wakes you up." This young man is that principle personified.

He learned many lessons while flying risky missions over enemy territory and he sent me a few that he thought could help healthcare professionals stand up to COVID-19. They apply to anyone doing high stakes, high pressure work. These are his words verbatim. My comments follow in italics.

NO FAST HANDS IN THE COCKPIT A misconception in the public is that the best fighter pilots must be those with lightning-fast reflexes. However, in reality, our training emphasizes just the opposite. During an inflight emergency, when the Master Caution light is flashing in your face, the urge to impulsively flip a switch or activate a back-up system can be overwhelming. It is during these moments that we fall back on our training, find the checklist that is the best fit for the scenario, and execute with deliberate focus. *When things get ugly, take a deep breath, and fall back on your training. Stick to the fundamentals.*

BOUNCE BACK Fighter pilots make mistakes all the time. Whether in dynamic training exercises or in actual combat, there is no shortage of threats that hinder perfect execution. The best among us are those who are able to acknowledge the mistake, mentally compartmentalize the error for the debrief, and continue the mission with a focus on all the other opportunities left to succeed on that sortie. *Rapid sequential tasking interrupted by generous self-affirmation is what our patients need from us.*

SHOW OF FORCE Unfortunately, in combat, the enemy gets a vote. This reality can produce moments of intense frustration when the circumstances of the engagement feel dictated by the adversary. In a tactical jet circling overhead as a chaotic ambush below unfolds, our most requested response is a "Show of Force." This maneuver calls for an extremely low, fast, and loud pass over the engagement and is intended to display to the enemy what a poor decision they just made. Although the desired response is a retreating enemy, often the feedback we receive is that of the uplifting effect the maneuver had on our friendly forces during their time of need. *There is no greater show of force than our dedicated teams of healthcare professionals bringing their best to the fore as we fight the battle of our lives.*

CHAPTER 63

THE POWER OF STORY

"We can survive the enemies at the gate, for they are known and carry banners. It is the enemy within that betrays us, his sly whispers rustling through the alleys of our minds."

—*Cicero and Taylor Caldwell, paraphrased*

The most important story in the world is the one we tell ourselves about ourselves. These stories have the power to keep us shackled in self-doubt and shame, or conversely, to liberate us to be our best selves. They include interpretations of our past, assessments of our present, and aspirations for our future. If you feel stuck in your life, the most productive thing you can do to get unstuck is to change your story. This in turn can change your habits, and those new habits will change your life.

Consider the story of the stonecutters. A man interviewed three stonecutters who were helping to build a temple. He asked each of them, "What are you doing?"

The first man was angry and answered, "Can't you see? I'm cutting rocks. I started as a child and will do this until I die."

The second man was smiling and replied, "I'm earning a living for my family."

The third man was radiant and exclaimed, "I'm building a place of worship where people can come to find hope and healing for hundreds of years."

Three men all doing the same work, but their self-stories changed their attitude and sense of joy and meaning.

I found a modern-day version of the stonecutters story on LinkedIn, a web-based professional networking site. A young woman posted that she was embarrassed about her college alma mater for many years because it was a local state school rather than a prestigious Ivy.

When I reviewed her resume, I saw a record of tremendous achievement that included holding part time jobs and completing competitive internships while attending her community college and state university. Her demonstrated ability to overcome numerous financial and social obstacles to earn a college degree demonstrated the type of character and grit I looked for when recruiting physicians for my medical group. Someone without a hint of entitlement or arrogance, who made the most of her circumstances and opportunities, and worked hard to better herself. While her shame eventually gave way to pride, some early positive counseling and a few encouraging words along the way could have saved her from years of unnecessary angst.

In stark contrast, another young woman who came from a similarly modest background posted her college to work story on LinkedIn but spent little time bemoaning her first generation status or lack of parental support for college tours and SAT prep courses. After a brief period of grieving the "unfairness" of her situation, she quickly realized that she needed to make the most of the opportunities she did have. She found out which schools were within her reach, worked extra hours to afford the gas to visit them, excelled in school, and ended up landing a fabulous job with a major entertainment company. Her conclusion about her life and experience: "Life is tough, but find the good where you can. #challenges #grateful."

Learning to tell ourselves a good story about ourselves comes easy to some, but for most, it's a struggle. Just because something makes common sense doesn't mean that it lends itself to common practice.

Mentors, counselors, and coaches play an important role in helping people to rewrite their stories. The goal is to produce legions of people who can look at themselves in the mirror and proclaim with conviction that they are smart enough, good enough, and fully worthy of love, belonging, and happiness.

For further reading on this topic, I recommend *The Little Engine That Could* by Arnold Monk. Those seeking a longer version of Monk's classic can check out *The Power of Story* by Jim Loehr.

CHAPTER 64

FOXHOLE MANTRAS

When leading resilience workshops, one of my favorite table activities is to have participants write down on a 3x5 index card the comment they repeat to themselves when the shit hits the fan. I call these "foxhole mantras," a reference to the words that come instinctively to soldiers hunkered down in a foxhole under a barrage of enemy fire. These dense nuggets of perspective and encouragement are oftentimes just what we need to pull us through a difficult situation. "This too shall end" (a reassuring reminder that most misery is finite) and "It could be worse" (a grateful acknowledgement that one could have fallen much deeper into the abyss of badness) are definitely in the top three. Also very popular are mantras laced with profanity, cursing being a time-honored way to vent anger and frustration when facing mayhem and the possibility of death.

Here are a few more foxhole mantras that I have heard and adopted for my personal use.

"THIS IS THE GAME, THE GAME IS HARD."—Jose Rosa Bonilla, M.D., emergency medicine. Dr. Bonilla reminds us that with responsibility comes hardship.

"I DON'T NEED EASY, I NEED POSSIBLE."—Jorge Gutierrez, Cal basketball player, 2008–2012

I was initiated to Cal sports in the fall of 1978 when a group of us living in Putnam Hall headed up the hill to Memorial Stadium on a sunny Saturday afternoon to watch our Bears play football against UCLA. In front of a national television audience, we threw TEN interceptions and lost 45-0. Over forty years later, I continue to follow and love my Bears, even though winning games is not our strong suit (unless you are talking about aquatic sports, which no one does unless it's a Summer Olympics year). For me, the best thing about Cal sports are the compelling stories of the student athletes. You may have heard of Marshawn Lynch and Aaron Rodgers (football), Jason Kidd and Jaylen Brown (basketball), Natalie Coughlin (swimming), Alex Morgan (soccer), and Collin Morikawa (golf).

My all-time favorite Cal student-athlete back story is that of Jorge Gutierrez, who played hoops at Cal from 2008–2012. Jorge grew up in Chihuahua, Mexico and fell in love with the game of basketball at a young age. Looking for an opportunity to improve his game and win a college scholarship, he snuck across the border illegally and settled in Denver where he excelled in high school basketball despite being malnourished and living in poverty with three other undocumented minors. He did not attract many recruiters and only ended up at Cal after another recruit backed out of his commitment. A relatively unremarkable athlete, he leveraged his work ethic and enthusiasm for the game to progress from a seldom-used substitute to Pac-12 Player of the Year as a senior. During his journey, he told a reporter, "I don't need easy, I need possible." In 2014 Gutierrez signed a contract with the Brooklyn Nets and became the fourth Mexican to play in the NBA.

"BE A SUGAR COOKIE." This comes from Navy SEALS training. SEALS are held to the highest standards of behavior and performance, including how well they maintain their uniforms. If they fail their uniform inspection, they are ordered to the beach to immerse themselves in the surf and then roll in the sand. They emerge looking like a cookie rolled in sugar and must wear their sandy crust like a scarlet letter for the rest of the day. This mantra is a reminder that oftentimes our best efforts are deemed not good enough, and that we must persevere in the face of judgement and shame.

"YOU DON'T HAVE TO FEEL GOOD TO DO GOOD." I had the pleasure of taking care of many couples during my career and "Jack" and "Judy" were among my favorites.

Jack was born the last of seven children into a poor immigrant family. His mother died of breast cancer when he was in the first grade. He had a gift for music and found comfort in playing the piano in his high school jazz band. He worked his way through law school playing music in nightclubs on the weekends. Soon after passing the bar, he met and married Judy and had a few kids.

Most of his friends were unaware that Jack had a case of major depression that dogged him his entire life. Maybe it stemmed from the trauma of losing his mother at a young age, but depression also ran strong in his family, so I'm sure genetics played a role. It wasn't bad enough to keep him from working, golfing, or fishing, but he lived most of his life with a negative self-narrative that was resistant to medications and counseling. Yet, his wife told me that if you ever went to one of Jack's extended family gatherings, you would never know that he was battling an inner demon. He was the first to compliment his nieces and nephews on their accomplishments, and when he sat down at the piano to play holiday songs, everyone gathered around him to bask in the glow of his goodness. If you had a problem, he was the first person to provide a listening ear, without a hint of judgement.

When I asked him how he was able to rise above his depression to be such a positive influence in the lives of others, he told me, "You don't have to feel good to do good."

"'NO' IS THE BEGINNING OF THE SALES CYCLE."—Jamie Brasseal (previously described as the most handsome and content man in the world).

I don't know much about sales, but I've read that there is an eight-step process that most successful salespeople are familiar with. Step 1 is prospecting. This is a fancy name for figuring out who you want to target for sales and procuring their contact information. Step 2 is connecting with your prospect and making a great first impression on them. Step 3 is qualifying your leads, which is a euphemism for separating the decision-makers from the wannabes.

Step 4 is delivering a product demonstration and making a compelling argument that your target needs what you have to offer. Your prospect will have doubts about your product, so Step 5 is addressing those concerns and reframing your pitch to reassure them you are the real deal.

Step 6 is to close the deal by getting them to sign a contract that begins the transfer of money to you and your product to them. If you are unable to close the deal, step 6b is to get the prospect to introduce you to the decision-maker they report to or another prospect who may need your services. Step 7 is handing off your client to your teammates who deliver the product. Step 8 is following up with your client to make sure that they are receiving everything you promised, and more.

Sounds simple enough, but how in the world does a salesperson maintain their self-respect when 99% of their prospects choose not to buy the product? Isn't it discouraging to have the door figuratively slammed on your face over and over again?

My poker buddy Jamie has enjoyed a long and successful career in sales and let me in on this sales secret that is not included in the eight-step sales cycle described above.

"No" is the beginning of the sales cycle.

What led him to say this with conviction? He pointed to the many lucrative contracts he had closed that started as firm "no's" from his prospects. He interpreted "no" as a challenge to better understand his client and return with a better pitch, not as an incrimination of him as a salesperson or human being.

Sounds like a positively adaptive attitude to have in life, regardless of whether or not you are in sales.

PART VI

DOCTOR STUFF

CHAPTER 65

YOUR BODY & BRAIN ONLY GET WORSE

*"The gentle downward slope gets steeper and
imperceptibly becomes an abyss."*

—*Tomas Tranströmer*

I was voted the most optimistic student in my Lowell High School graduating class of 850 students. Some people thought I was naive, but the truth was that I saw a lot of bad stuff while growing up in San Francisco (think the Zodiac killer and the assassinations of Supervisor Harvey Milk and Mayor George Moscone). I decided that if life was going to dish out badness, I was going to focus on the positive and help others do the same.

With that perspective firmly established, I knew from the beginning that my responsibility as a physician was not to save people from dying, because we all must die, but rather to maximize their health and longevity and minimize their suffering as they navigated their inevitable decline and eventual death. To borrow a phrase from Atul Gawande's *Being Mortal*, my job was to help "people in a state of dependence sustain the value of existence."

Why can't human beings live forever? Single-celled organisms like bacteria live to a certain age and then divide into two healthy bacteria without any step off in virility. Strawberries grow runners underground and create clones of themselves. And neither of them have access to alkaline water or Pilates training.

We are not so lucky. Our cells are programmed to divide about 50 times, and then die. Aging experts think that our mortality is driven by numerous factors that accumulate over time to compromise the integrity of the molecules, cells, and organs that make up our being. A primary culprit is the deterioration of our genetic code. That code is found in our DNA, and that DNA is constantly at risk of being damaged or modified by spontaneous mutations, harmful chemical compounds such as free radicals, and faulty copying during cell division. Over time, waste products build up within cells and this prevents normal energy metabolism. Our body's immune system wanes over time, fails in its old age to recognize and destroy dangerous foreign invaders, and sometimes gets confused and attacks our own cells and organs. You get the picture, and it's not so pretty.

In my practice, the three most common age-related issues I help patients to cope with are the narrowing of blood vessels, the reduction of joint spaces, and the deterioration of brain function. Because of preventive healthcare (think fluoride to prevent dental caries and vaccinations to prevent smallpox), most of us will live long enough to suffer the ravages of these conditions.

ATHEROSCLEROSIS The process by which our blood vessels become narrower and stiffer over time is called atherosclerosis. The buildup of cholesterol, fats, and other substances leads to plaque formation in the lining of blood vessels. These plaques reduce the vessels' effective diameter and the amount of oxygen-rich life-sustaining blood they can deliver to their end organs. Plaques usually build up slowly and gradually diminish blood supply, but they can also rupture and cause clots that suddenly and completely obstruct a blood vessel.

Either way, atherosclerosis starves vital organs of the blood they need to survive leading to strokes, heart attacks and heart failure, kidney failure, and cold and painful extremities (a condition known as peripheral vascular disease). The reduced elasticity of aging blood vessels leads to increased pressure in the vascular system, which explains in large part why high blood pressure is present in two-thirds of people over age 65.

DEGENERATIVE ARTHRITIS For our joints to work properly, they must maintain the space between bones that allows for painless range of motion. The narrowing of joint spaces, and associated compression and damage of the cartilage that protects the articulating surface of bones from grinding against one another, goes by the names degenerative arthritis, osteoarthritis, and wear-and-tear arthritis.

It most notably affects the gravity-sensitive weight-bearing hips, knees, and spine and our precious hands that we use to grip, grasp, and execute fine movements such as writing, texting, and sewing. Doctors perform 500,000 hip replacements and nearly 1,000,000 knee replacements per year in the United States so that people hobbled by arthritis can literally rise up and walk again. By the year 2040, those numbers are projected to skyrocket to 1,500,000 and 3,500,000 respectively. At this time, such straightforward and successful treatment options are not available for the hands and back.

Patients who have degenerative arthritis come to see me with complaints of pain with an activity that was previously enjoyed pain free. Oftentimes they are people who have subjected their joints to substantial stress (think former high school athletes and those with manual labor jobs).

They frequently tell me, "But doctor, I've never had this pain before." To which my reply is, "That may be true, but you have it now."

MEMORY LOSS & DEMENTIA The most stressful part of aging is related to the decline of the captain of our ship, the human brain. This three-pound powerhouse of interconnected neurons is so precious that it comes with its own high-quality football helmet, the skull. While it comprises only 2% of our body weight, the brain consumes 20% of our daily calories as it performs the following tasks: interpreting all forms of sensory input; determining and executing our responses; and processing a wide range of thoughts and emotions that span from fight or flight responses to danger, navigating new romantic relationships, and calculating the wave angle for a given Mach and deflection angle in an oblique shock.

Somewhere in our mid 40s, we start to experience normal age-related changes in brain function. It takes longer to learn new things, we have trouble remembering people's names, and we keep losing our keys. About 40% of people age 65 or older have this age-related memory impairment. About 10% of people age 65 or older have a more severe form of memory loss called mild cognitive impairment which is hallmarked by memory loss with relative sparing of function. Each year, 15% of these people progress to having dementia, the most serious form of brain decline in which memory loss is accompanied by a loss of the brain and body functions essential for safe and independent living.

Here are some other signs and symptoms of our bodies and brains getting worse over time, all of which keep me very busy as a family physician.

ITCHY, THIN, BLEEDING, WEEPY SKIN Skin protects our body from the environment, helps to regulate our body temperature, provides a lattice for the nerves that provide sensory input to our brain, and in combination with our body habitus, clothes, and other adornments, provides a total visual package that others use to formulate first impressions about us.

We don't really think about it until something goes wrong with its function or appearance (think pimples, poison oak, hair loss, and skin cancer).

Like many of my patients, I enjoyed carefree good skin for decades. Then at age 50, things went south. As if someone had flipped a switch during my sleep, my skin began to itch from my scalp to my toes. Years of shampooing my hair daily and taking long hot showers had sucked my skin dry of the fat and moisture required to keep it healthy.

In order to continue living comfortably in my skin, I had to follow the advice I regularly dished out to my patients: take short tepid showers, shampoo only twice weekly, and limit the use of a nice moisturizing soap to the armpits, groin, and feet. Then within a minute of patting dry with a towel, seal in the moisture by applying liberal amounts of creams for the hands and feet, and lotions for the rest of the body.

What further deterioration do I have to look forward to in the future? My skin will become progressively thin and fragile, taking on the appearance of crepe paper, as its middle layer, the dermis, produces less of the collagen that gives it strength and the elastin that keeps it taut. If I live long enough, my sagging skin will reveal its underlying unsightly veins and tendons, and bleed easily with the slightest of provocations, such as brushing up against a wall, resulting in the massive black, blue, and purple bruises seen in the arms and hands of our grandparents.

At some point, the skin overlying my legs and feet will accumulate visible fluid by the end of each day, a condition called dependent edema, due to a combination of gravity and the diminished ability of the veins and lymphatic system to return upstream to the heart the blood and fluid it sent to the feet throughout the day. This fluid accumulation can be mild (leaving the familiar sock mark impressions), moderate (giving your skin a doughy consistency in which you can leave divots with sustained thumb pressure, a condition known as pitting edema), and severe (where the pressure exerted by the swelling is so severe that it causes skin breakdown and the weeping of fluid).

HEARING LOSS One third of people aged 65–75 have some degree of hearing loss and after age 75 that number goes up to more than half. Hearing is a complicated process that begins with sound waves hitting the eardrum and being conducted through the tiny bones of the middle ear to the inner ear. Delicate hair cells in the inner ear translate those vibrations into electrical signals that are transmitted to the brain where they are interpreted and perceived as sound. With time, the ability to conduct sound vibrations, turn them into electrical signals, and then interpret those signals wanes. Genetics, exposure to noise, and some medications can contribute to this decline.

VISION LOSS By age 65, approximately one third of people have some sort of vision-reducing disease for a wide variety of reasons. Cataracts, opacities that develop in the lens located in the front of the eye, keep light signals from reaching the retina, the light sensing tissue located in the back of the eye. Presbyopia is caused by an aging lens losing its ability to flex and change its shape to focus on close-up images. Glaucoma is a condition in which increased pressure in the eye causes damage to the optic nerve that connects the eye to the brain, resulting in vision loss and sometimes blindness. Age-related macular degeneration (AMD) damages the part of the retina responsible for central vision. The elevated blood sugars associated with diabetes can damage the small blood vessels that nourish the retina, causing them to leak fluid and further impair vision. All in all, it's not a pretty picture, and it gets darker and murkier with each passing day.

DIGESTIVE PROBLEMS The gut is one continuous muscular tube that starts at the lips and ends at the anus. Plus, as I was astonished to learn in medical school, the contents of its lining actually lie exterior to the body proper. Had I decided to subspecialize in medicine, gastroenterology would have been my choice. In addition to being a logical next step to my undergraduate degree in nutrition, the specialty involves many interesting procedures.

The function of the mouth and teeth is to mechanically break down food into smaller pieces that are then lubricated with saliva, tossed back into the back of the throat by the tongue, and then massaged into the stomach by the esophagus. Of note, the active propulsion of food in the esophagus is what allows you to swallow a cookie while standing on your head.

In the stomach muscle, the proteins, fats, carbohydrates, vitamins, minerals, and water that make up the meal are churned further, bathed in acid, and then sent downstream into the small intestines as a slurry called chyme. The chyme is mixed further in a medley of enzymes and bile acids produced by the liver, pancreas, and intestines. This produces tiny particles of nutrients (such as amino acids, fatty acids, glycerol, and sugars) that the intestines absorb and deliver to the appropriate destinations in the body. That which is not absorbed is sent downstream into the colon where much of its water content is reabsorbed before being passed through the anus as stool.

Between the lips and anus lie numerous opportunities for digestive misery. Reflux is a condition in which corrosive stomach acids escape upwards into the esophagus, resulting in a burning sensation in the lining of the esophagus (thus the term "heartburn"). This acid can disrupt the esophagus' ability to massage food downstream, resulting in swallowing problems.

Gallstones are solidified concretions of digestive juices found in the gallbladder. They range in size from a grain of sand to a golf ball. If larger stones get stuck in one of the ducts that drain contents of the gallbladder and pancreas into the intestines, they cause severe crampy pain, especially in the wake of fatty meals that stimulate the gallbladder to contract.

Constipation is defined as a distressful reduction in bowel movements (usually less than three per week) and/or having difficulty passing stools. While the cause is sometimes identifiable and easily corrected (dehydration, inadequate dietary fiber, physical inactivity, and medication-associated come to mind), most cases related to aging have no identifiable causes other than the colon getting weak and lazy about its essential functions of optimizing the formation, storage, and passage of stool.

Constipation leads to straining at stool, which in turn causes veins in the rectum (internal hemorrhoids) and under the skin around the anus (external hemorrhoids) to distend, bleed, and in the case of external hemorrhoids, hurt.

How miserable can constipation be? So bad that one of my most experienced and esteemed colleagues in medicine referred to it as "the worst problem ever."

Additional age-related disorders of the rectum and anal sphincter muscle include incontinence of stool, impaction of stool, anal fissures (painful cuts in the skin of the anal canal), and rectal prolapse, a condition in which the rectum slides out of the anus.

Though it is not an age-related disorder, I must mention irritable bowel syndrome (IBS), a painful condition that affects ten percent of the elderly and accounts for ten percent of visits to a primary care physician and thirty percent of referrals to gastroenterologists. IBS is a diagnosis of exclusion and is hallmarked by recurrent severe abdominal pain that has no identifiable cause. Common signs and symptoms include bloating, constipation, diarrhea, the sensation of incomplete emptying of the colon and rectum with bowel movements, and difficulty sleeping.

The cause of this prevalent condition cannot be found by endoscopic examinations of the gut, imaging studies, or tests of the blood and stool, and there are no simple cures. In my practice, the majority of "severe" cases of abdominal pain turn out to be irritable bowel.

GENITOURINARY SAGGING, LEAKS AND DRIBBLES The male and female genitourinary systems are arguably the most mixed bags of joy, pleasure, and misery in the human body. What was our creator's reasoning for intertwining our sexual organs with the urinary plumbing? How can it be that the penis, a man's aroused vector for life-spawning ejaculate, also serves as the expressway for urine making a B-line for the outside world? Similarly, one would think that the ultimate architect might have found someplace other than just north of the vagina as the location for the urethral meatus through which urine exits the female body.

In their youth, men enjoy the quadfecta of a healthy libido, firm erections, bladders that can store a large amount of urine without complaint, and a strong urinary flow. That's why they can go to a football game, drink eight beers over the first three quarters of the game, pee just once in the fourth quarter (with a stream strong enough to span the ten yards required to get a first down), and then while inebriated, have sex twice before passing out.

Male testosterone production peaks in the late teens, plateaus for a couple of decades, then begins to decline in the fourth decade of life. With that decline comes nothing good. Libido, sexual function, bone density, and lean body mass all wane. With age, the bladder gets stiffer, weaker, and twitchier, resulting in more frequent trips to the bathroom.

Urinary problems are further compounded by changes in the prostate gland which sits just below the bladder. When young and healthy, the prostate gland is the size of a golf ball and produces much of the fluid found in semen. It also serves two muscular functions: to push its fluids into the urethra for ejaculation and to close off the connection to the bladder so that ejaculate is not diluted with urine. With age, the prostate gland can double in size and squeeze on the urethra that passes through its core, resulting in a diminished urinary stream. This explains why young men can pee with the force of a fire hose and old men dribble urine onto their shoes.

Women are most fertile in their late teens and twenties, during which time they experience a monthly cycling of hormones that results in the release of an egg from one of their ovaries into the fallopian tube. During this phase of their lives, the likelihood of the following cascade of events is at its peak: ovulation of a healthy egg, fertilization of that egg by sperm in the fallopian tube, implantation of the fertilized egg in the lining of the uterus, and the steady maturation of the embryo to a fetus to a healthy newborn.

Late in the third decade of life, the ovaries start to produce less estrogen and progesterone which in turn leads to a reduction in ovulation and fertility.

In the fourth decade, the reduced hormone levels also cause irregular menses, vaginal dryness, breast sagging and tenderness, hot flashes, disrupted sleep, mood changes, and weight gain.

Advancing age is also associated with a weakening and relaxation of the muscles and ligaments that hold up the bladder, uterus, vagina, and rectum, resulting in the southerly gravity-driven migration of those organs into public places they should not be. This can cause pain with intercourse and incontinence of urine and stool.

I vividly remember a case of prolapse from my medical student rotation on the inpatient gynecology ward. One of our patients was an elderly woman whose chief complaint was, "I'm growing a penis." The tip of her uterus and its central os (the small opening that leads to the body of the uterus) had dropped low enough to protrude from her vagina, and it resembled the glans of a penis and its centrally located urethra.

FRAILTY The end result of our body's decline is frailty, a state of increased vulnerability to acute and chronic challenges to our health and survival. In addition to the laundry list of aforementioned indignities, we must rally to adapt to a decline in the flexibility, strength, and balance required to carry out activities of daily living (ADLs) such as bathing, dressing, and transferring out of bed and chairs.

About 15% of people aged 55–64 have difficulty with such basic daily activities and this number goes up to 25% in those 65 and older. About one third of people age 65 and older report difficulty with walking a few blocks or going up one flight of stairs and one fifth require the use of an assistive device to get around. By age 85, up to half of us are classified as frail, and this puts us at increased risk for falls, disability, long term care, and death.

When patients press me for the main drivers of frailty and their transition from independence to dependence, I list the following: arthritis which limits our range of motion; the loss of muscle mass and strength; deterioration of the balance centers in our inner ear and brain; a decline in our nervous system's ability to send us signals about our position in space; and a blunted compensatory response by our heart and peripheral blood vessels when we transition from sitting or lying to standing, resulting in light headedness, and in extreme cases, loss of consciousness.

DEATH My first remembrances of death were associated with my childhood pet goldfish and hamsters. While I was sad, I recovered quickly, mostly because we would just go to the pet store and replace them.

The passing of my maternal grandfather, Albert Jing, was completely different.

I was eight years old when my mother received a phone call informing her that he had died from a massive stroke. His service was held at the First Chinese Baptist Church in Fresno. I remember filing past his open casket where I saw him lying motionless, a calm expression on his face, elbows bent so that his hands could rest comfortably, one on top of the other on his belly—and the lowering of his casket into the ground at the Belmont Memorial Park.

The melancholy of our family's mourning was captured in a ballad of that period, Simon and Garfunkel's *Scarborough Fair*. And while my parents did a good job of comforting and coaching me through the experience, my fears about death were stoked by my viewing of *Dark Shadows*, ABC's gothic daytime soap that featured stories of witches, warlocks, zombies, and vampire Barnabus Collins rising out of a casket.

Fast forward to medical school at UCLA fourteen years later where I was immersed in a crash course on death that featured dissecting a lifeless body in gross anatomy; observing autopsies of the first AIDS victims; using a microscope to see the magnified details of disease and destruction; building relationships with sick patients, many of whom would succumb to their chronic condition, such as diabetes, or their acute illnesses, such as an overwhelming pneumococcal bacterial infection; fatal car accidents involving drunk drivers; and gunshot and knife wound victims.

I remember well the first patient I pronounced dead as a newly minted physician. I was an intern doing an overnight on-call shift at the UC Davis Medical Center and was paged by a nurse on the East 8 medical/surgical ward to evaluate a terminally ill patient who was found motionless and unresponsive. A code blue was not called because the patient and his family had requested no heroic interventions in the event of his natural death.

I pulled back the curtain that the nurse had closed to shield the newly-deceased from his roommates. I saw a slender, older male lying peacefully in bed with his eyes closed. I had reviewed the protocol for pronouncing a human being dead: confirm the patient's identity; check for the absence of a pupillary response to light; check for a response to stimuli; check with a stethoscope for heart sounds and with fingers for pulses over the major arteries; and finally, observe for spontaneous respirations.

The last step is trickier than it sounds. As patients approach death, they sometimes exhibit Cheyne-Stokes breathing, an irregular pattern and cadence of respiration that can include long periods of complete stillness between breaths. The last thing a young and inexperienced intern wants is to be ridiculed as the doctor who pronounced a patient dead, only to have that patient "come alive" in the morgue.

So I observed the patient for several minutes before convincing myself that he was dead. All the while, my imagination got the better of me and saw subtle spontaneous chest movements where there were none.

The next steps were to notify the family of his passing (an emotional and delicate conversation, especially when covering for a colleague) and to write a death note in the medical chart (a task that would become rote in the years to follow but which I always carried out with a sense of solemnity and respect for the patient and their survivors).

Over my career, I became increasingly familiar with the wide variety of causes and circumstances of death. In addition to those previously mentioned: infertility (to those afflicted, as real as any death); fetal demise; severe birth defects incompatible with life; childhood trauma and abuse; mental health disorders leading to homicide and suicide; substance abuse, most notably involving alcohol and narcotics; heart attacks and heart failure; strokes; progressive neurologic disease such as Parkinson's and amyotrophic lateral sclerosis (Lou Gehrig's disease); lung disease such as emphysema; autoimmune disease in which the body's immune system turns against self, such as lupus; and cancers of all types including carcinomas of organs and glands (think prostate, breast, lung, and colon), sarcomas (cancer of the connective tissues including bone and muscle), leukemia (cancer of the blood), and lymphoma (cancer of the lymphatic system that fights infection).

Regardless of the details, the end result was always the same: the beating heart and warm moist breath of a living being ceased, and in the cases of those who made it past childhood, a human being who was once walking, talking, working, laughing, singing, eating, and loving, crossed over a one-way threshold to a new state of stillness and quiet, never again to smile, offer a kind word, return a warm embrace, or attend a gathering of family and friends. No more wrapping or opening presents, writing or reading letters, sharing inside jokes, taking out Chinese food, enjoying a hot dog and peanuts at a baseball game, building sand castles at the beach, or planting bulbs and waiting for them to bloom.

An awareness of the certainty of death and the uncertainty of its timing is a double-edged sword. On one hand, it can foster overwhelming anxiety, despair, and inaction. Why bother to even try making something of our lives if the details are out of our control, and regardless of what we do, we end up dying anyway?

Conversely, a consistent awareness of our mortality, the relative brevity of our existence, and the possibility that this day could be our last has the power to foster a healthy attitude of making the most of every day. People who live with this perspective approach life with a reality-based framework that focuses on gratitude, big picture dreams, and putting in the work to make those dreams come true.

CHAPTER 66

IT'S MOSTLY ABOUT
LIFESTYLE CHOICES

*"I should indeed like to please you; but I prefer to save you,
whatever your attitude be toward me."*

—*Daniel Webster to his constituents*

Those of us who live in Western societies have run ourselves ragged with bad choices about food, activity, and mental health. Our widespread consumption of inexpensive, convenient, tasty food with low nutritional value, sedentary lifestyles that favor sitting and lounging over movement, and disregard for our emotional health directly lead to chronic illnesses such as cardiovascular disease, cancer, obesity, and type 2 diabetes. These chronic conditions are the primary drivers of our sickness (morbidity), death (mortality), and healthcare costs.

The numbers are staggering. Nearly one million Americans per year die from heart disease or stroke (accounting for one third of all deaths), costing the healthcare system $215B/year and $140B/year in lost productivity. Every year, 1.7 million Americans are diagnosed with cancer and 600,000 of us die from it. The annual cost of treating these cancers is $175B and rising. Thirty-five million Americans have diabetes and the combined cost of their medical care and lost productivity is $327B/year. Another 88 million have prediabetes, a condition of high blood sugars that is a risk factor for diabetes, heart disease, and stroke. Forty percent of adult and twenty percent of children are obese, putting them at risk for diabetes, heart disease, and some cancers and the treatment of obesity costs $150B/year.

Despite the fact that the United States spends more money per capita on healthcare than any other developed nation ($11,000 per person in 2019 or 17% of our GDP; the next closest is Switzerland at $7700 per person or 12.1% of GDP), we have the highest chronic disease burden, the highest rates of hospitalizations from preventable diseases such as diabetes and heart disease, and the lowest life expectancy. Our prevailing model of fee-for-service medical care is largely to blame for this poor return on investment. By paying healthcare providers and hospitals more to treat sick people than we pay them to keep healthy people well, we effectively incentivize sick care over preventive care.

The solution to this dilemma lies in shifting our focus and resources from the drugs, dialysis machines, and bypass surgeries that treat the ravages of chronic conditions to the adoption of the proactive preventive care recommendations that prevent these chronic conditions from happening in the first place. An ounce of prevention is worth a pound of cure, and then some. It should also be noted that a focus on prevention works best when coupled with a prepaid integrated system of care where the patients, providers, and hospitals all benefit from the patients being healthy rather than sick. Failure to orchestrate that alignment of incentives between the payers, providers, and recipients of care will result in a continuation of the frustrating high cost and maddeningly mediocre outcome system we are saddled with now.

The emerging specialty of lifestyle medicine nicely groups preventive practices into the "four quadrants of total health": healthy eating; active living; healthy weight; and emotional resilience.

HEALTHY EATING A whole food plant based diet has been proven to control, improve, and even reverse many chronic conditions. Whole foods are natural foods that have not been heavily processed. Plant based means from plants without the addition of animal based products such as meat, milk, eggs, and honey. After attending a plant based nutrition conference that featured presentations by experts in the field and plant based meals, I learned that a diet of fruits, vegetables, tubers, whole grains, and legumes can be not only nutritious and health promoting, but also delicious and satisfying. However, it should be noted that the adherence to an exclusively plant based diet is a hurdle of herculean proportions, and for many people like me, it will never be an absolute. In fact, three days into the course, I ditched the repetitive vegan dinner buffet and snuck away to a nearby Chinese restaurant to indulge in a meal of fish steamed with black beans, ginger, and green onions. The way I see it, I can live with Meatless Mondays and Tofu Tuesdays indefinitely. But in the one life I have to live, I'm not going to forever exclude the occasional celebratory dim sum, grilled steak, or ice cream cone just to extend my golden years (because take it from a pro, those golden years ain't always so golden).

Active Living Years ago, for our 25th wedding anniversary, my wife and I took our two kids on a two-week vacation to London and Paris.

In London, we gorged ourselves daily at our hotel's full English breakfast and then ventured out to various neighborhoods to sample fish and chips, bangers and mash, shepherd's pie, and of course, the ever-present Indian cuisine.

In Paris, we feasted on croissants, baguettes, cheese, chocolates, macaroons, and falafels with fries. Yet despite our high caloric diets, none of us gained any weight on the trip. The reason is that along with the natives of London and Paris, we got around by using public transportation and walking. I didn't have an Apple watch at the time, but I would guess that we logged an average of 15,000 to 25,000 steps/day which included lots of stairs and some hills.

Compare that to my 2000 steps/day lifestyle in the United States where I get in my car, drive to work, walk about a half block from the parking lot into my clinic, see patients (which involves going back and forth from my office to the exam rooms about 20–25 times/day), walk back to my car, drive home, and settle down for a sedentary evening. Thus the need for those with sedentary work and home lives to actively engage in movement programs. It really doesn't matter exactly what you do to move, but if you like the activity, you are much more likely to make it a habit.

For example, I don't like to run, and I can say with absolute certainty that I've never experienced the "runner's high." Conversely, I can walk a long way and enjoy every step of the journey. I've told my family on many occasions that my enjoyment of walking makes me think that I may be the descendent of a long line of mail carriers in China.

So for the past two decades, with no prompting necessary, I have walked on a very consistent basis (and actually feel bad when I don't). You might feel the same way about gardening, rowing, biking, or doing high intensity training at the gym. Whatever floats your boat. But do keep that boat afloat.

HEALTHY WEIGHT The Body Mass Index (BMI) is used widely to assess an individual's weight and health. BMI is a person's weight in kilograms divided by height in meters squared. A BMI of less than 18.5 falls within the underweight range; 18.5 to 24.9 within the normal or healthy weight range; 25.0 to 29.9 within the overweight range; and 30.0 or higher within the obese range. The problem with the BMI is that it does not take into account the source of the weight (e.g. lean muscle, bone, or fat) or the type of fat (white, brown, beige, subcutaneous, or visceral). A very fit athlete with dense bones and generous amounts of lean muscle can have a high BMI in the obese range and a slender sedentary person with high amounts of dangerous visceral fat ("belly fat") can have a BMI in the healthy range. When counseling patients, I advise them that BMI is just one number that we use to assess their body composition.

Emotional Resilience Stress, anxiety, and depression are commonplace in society and patients often turn to their healthcare providers for relief from their emotional pain. In 2019, nearly 20% of Americans received treatment for their mental health, 16% took medications for the same, and 10% received counseling or therapy from a mental health professional. Emotional resilience is the ability to bounce back from adverse situations and return to a baseline state of health. Building and maintaining it is essential to a life well lived.

Can lifestyle practices actually promote longevity and good health? In a 2009 article titled "Healthy Living Is The Best Revenge" published in the *Archives of Internal Medicine*, Ford, Bergmann, *et al* described a European prospective study of 23,000 participants who were instructed to adhere to four simple recommendations: No tobacco use, 30 minutes of exercise five times per week, maintaining a BMI of less than 30 kg/m^2, and eating a healthy diet. Participants who adhered to these four recommendations had an overall 78% decreased risk of development of a chronic condition during an eight-year timeframe. Furthermore, in participants adhering to these recommendations, there was a 93% reduced risk of diabetes mellitus, an 81% reduced risk of myocardial infarction, and a 36% reduction in the risk of the development of cancer.

Further evidence of the positive effects of healthy lifestyle choices can be found in The Blue Zones, five regions of the world described by Dan Buettner where people live longer healthier lives. They are Okinawa, Japan; Sardinia, Italy; Nicoya, Costa Rica; Icaria, Greece; and the Seventh-day Adventist community in Loma Linda, California. While these communities are geographically and culturally diverse, their people share the following health-promoting lifestyle habits: abstinence from smoking; moderate regular physical activity; living for a purpose; stress reduction; moderate caloric intake; plant based diets; moderate alcohol intake; and engagement in spirituality/religion, family life, and social life.

CHAPTER 67

THE KING OF ALL HEALTH

Cardiologists think of the heart as the most important driver of health. After all, if the heart is not healthy enough to efficiently pump blood to the cells of the body, those cells die.

Similarly, Dan Henry, a nephrologist and my medical school instructor in the fundamentals of clinical medicine, held up the kidneys as the kings of our castles. He persuasively argued that if the kidneys did not perform their function of removing metabolic waste and maintaining a steady state of water, salts, and minerals, we would surely balloon up and die.

The truth is that every medical subspecialist can make a strong argument for their piece of the puzzle being the most important. In fact, humans are made up of many parts, and we are at our best when all of those parts are working in a coordinated fashion with one another.

That being said, there are subjective hierarchies in life. The late Alain Renoir, UC Berkeley professor emeritus of English, son of the great film director/producer Jean Renoir, and grandson of the impressionist painter Pierre-Auguste Renoir, told me that among academics at Cal, there was a well-established intellectual pecking order that placed mathematicians at the top, English professors in the middle, and psychologists at the bottom. *Note: I never shared this assessment with my late father, who as noted earlier, was a psychology major at Cal and fancied himself as intellectually robust.*

Back to the subject of health, as I step back and look at the lives of my patients, friends, and family, as well as my own life, my vote for the most important type of health is (drumroll please)...mental health. What is mental health?

According to the United States Office of Disease Prevention & Health Promotion, "Mental health is a state of successful performance of mental function, resulting in productive activities, fulfilling relationships with other people, and the ability to adapt to change and to cope with challenges. Mental health is essential to personal well-being, family and interpersonal relationships, and the ability to contribute to community or society. Mental disorders are health conditions that are characterized by alterations in thinking, mood, and/or behavior that are associated with distress and/or impaired functioning. Mental disorders contribute to a host of problems that may include disability, pain, or death."

Having good mental health is the gateway to enjoying all other types of good health. It empowers you to make good decisions about lifestyle, relationships, work, and leisure. It gives you the capacity to make plans, be flexible, and effectively adapt to change. It gifts you with the curiosity to discover the people and world outside of you, the capacity to introspectively explore what you want your life to be all about, and the determination and perseverance to then venture out of your apartment and make it happen.

> *"Mental illness is the pandemic of the 21st century and will be*
> *the next major global health challenge."*
> —*Drs. James Lake & Mason Spain Turner*

But good mental health is elusive. Fifty percent of adults will be diagnosed with a mental illness at some point in their lifetime. In any given year, roughly 44 million Americans carry a diagnosis of mental illness, and for nearly 10 million of them, that illness is seriously debilitating. Suicide is the tenth leading cause of death in the United States, and takes the lives of 40,000 people per year, more than a maximum capacity crowd at Fenway Park (which tops out at 38,000). Psychological disorders are the leading cause of disability, accounting for 20% of years of life lost to disability and premature death.

The prospects for a brighter tomorrow are bleak. Even after a mental health disorder is diagnosed, access to the appropriate care and the effectiveness of that care is inconsistent and unpredictable, due to the numerous biological, social, cultural, and spiritual determinants of mental health. Unlike many other types of medical problems, the powerful and persistent thoughts and feelings associated with mental health disorders seldom respond to quick fixes.

What we do have as treatment options are psychotropic medications (drugs like Valium and Prozac that affect a person's mental state), psychotherapeutic interventions (examples being cognitive behavioral therapy and insight oriented therapy), and in some cases, electroconvulsive therapy, transcranial magnetic stimulation, or ketamine infusions.

Some people are literally born with mental health disorders due to strong family histories, genetic predispositions, and *in utero* exposure to toxins, alcohol, and drugs. Once born, poverty, childhood abuse or neglect, stressful life situations, traumatic experiences, isolation and loneliness, and once again, alcohol and drugs can take a bad situation and make it worse.

Anxiety disorders are the most common type of mental health disorders and involve sustained or recurrent anxiety, worry, or fear that are out of proportion to the actual danger.

Examples include generalized anxiety disorder (excessive anxiety or worry on most days for six months or more about what most would perceive as ordinary issues related to everyday life), panic attacks (triggered or inexplicable sudden-onset attacks of intense fear that peak within minutes), and phobias (irrational or excessive fear of specific triggers such as people or situations that they believe put them at risk for failure, shame, or harm).

Mood disorders are characterized by sustained emotional states and moods that are distorted or inconsistent with one's circumstances and that interfere with one's ability to perform essential functions such as work, raising a family, and completing routine daily activities.

Examples include major depressive disorder (recurrent prolonged periods of extreme sadness and loss of interest in usual activities), dysthymia (a sustained low grade depression or irritable mood that lasts more than two years), seasonal affective disorder (aka SAD, associated with fewer daylight hours in the late fall and early spring), bipolar disorder (aka manic depression, characterized by extreme high and lows in mood), and depression related to medical conditions, prescription medications, or substance abuse.

Personality disorders involve rigid and dysfunctional ways of thinking and behaving. Subtypes include schizoid (difficulty picking up social cues; appearance of being indifferent; and a preference for being alone); antisocial (disregard for others' needs and feelings; lying, stealing, and trouble with the law; impulsive with a disregard for safety); borderline (fragile self-image, labile mood; unstable relationships; fear of abandonment); narcissistic (exaggerated sense of self-importance; constant yearning of attention and praise; unreasonable expectation of returned favors); dependent (lack of self-confidence and excessive need to be taken care of; clingy behavior; tolerance of abuse); and obsessive-compulsive (rigid, stubborn, and preoccupied with rules and perfectionism; intolerance of dissimilar beliefs and values).

Those of you who are living with one of these conditions, or have a family member or close friend so afflicted, understand how they can cast a dark shadow over every aspect of one's life. Mood, anxiety, and personality disorders can wreak havoc on family dynamics, workplace productivity, and the overall camaraderie and safety of a community. Hypertension, diabetes, and heart disease can't hold a candle to major depression, panic disorder, and antisocial personality when it comes to seeding loneliness, heartbreak, and carnage.

Is there any hope on the horizon for improved mental health for human beings?

Given my bias about the paramount importance of mental health, I'm pleased to share my opinion that the answer is an enthusiastic "Yes!"

The first step is to build on existing efforts to destigmatize mental health disorders and the use of mental health professionals.

My personal contribution to the effort is to publicly share and endorse my own positive experience with mental health counseling. As part of a pilot physician wellness experiment, my office colleagues and I were enrolled in a series of counseling sessions through our employee assistance program (EAP).

My counselor was Marissa Pierce, a licensed marriage and family therapist. Our meetings were friendly and helpful. I didn't have to lay down on a couch, and she wasn't wearing a tweed sport coat or smoking a pipe.

More than anything else, I found Marissa to be a calm and empathetic listener, and I trusted that given her professional background and inside scoop on the life experiences and self-stories of thousands of patients, she was providing me with not only advice, but also a sage perspective about how my life fit into the overall picture of the human experience.

Whenever someone asked me what Marissa did for me, my reply was, "She keeps me more right in the head."

When I give wellness talks, I always include a snapshot of Marissa and me during a counseling session, and I implore people to engage in counseling not only for themselves, but as a gift to all the people in their lives. It's part of my public service announcement (PSA) campaign to change the conversation and beliefs about mental health and the benefits of counseling. My goal is to get people to a point where they are just as proud and enthusiastic about publicly praising their therapist as they are about talking up their Cross Fit coach, hair stylist, and personal vegan chef.

The importance and effectiveness of this message was made clear to me several years ago when a colleague shared a story with me at the end of a wellness session I led for his department.

He said that five years earlier, he attended one of my presentations in which I showed the "Marissa Pierce & Me" slide and encouraged the audience to pursue counseling to improve their mental health. He explained that at that time, his life was in disarray and he was contemplating taking his own life. Had he successfully carried out his plan, he would have joined the 300–400 American physicians who successfully kill themselves every year.

Prompted by my simple suggestion, he reached out to EAP and began a counseling relationship that allowed him to deal with his issues and get his life back on track.

I had two immediate thoughts about his story. The first was an affirmation of my belief that we need to talk more openly and freely about our mental health issues. The second and overwhelmingly discouraging thought was this: "How sick is our prevailing culture that another human being believed he needed permission from me to seek help for his suicidal thoughts?"

The answer is…super sick.

The time to change a culture that shames people who are living with depression, anxiety, and other psychiatric problems is now. Lives are literally at stake if we fail to immediately right this wrong.

If we can get people to buy into counseling, the next challenge is the current and anticipated future shortage of mental health providers (defined here as psychiatrists; clinical, counseling, and school psychologists; mental health and substance abuse social workers; school counselors; and marriage and family therapists) as well as the primary care providers (family physicians, internists, pediatricians, ob/gyns, nurse practitioners, and physician assistants) who play a major role in the initial evaluation of mental health disorders and often provided ongoing care, especially in more rural areas where mental health specialists are scare.

The answer to this manpower shortage and maldistribution lies in more collaborative models of care that recruit non-traditional providers to be part of the solution. These models are team-driven, population-focused, measurement-guided, and evidence-based. They welcome with open arms complementary and alternative medicine (CAM) and integrative medicine, two movements that were formerly considered fringe, but are now touted as part of the cavalry riding into town to close the gap between a community's mental health needs and the capacity of that community to meet those needs.

A growing body of evidence supports the safety and efficacy of CAM treatments such as pharmaceutical-grade natural products, lifestyle modifications, mind-body approaches, and Eastern based whole-system approaches (such as Chinese medicine and Ayurveda).

Integrative medicine is an inclusive model of care that recognizes both the importance of traditional Western allopathic care and CAM while thoughtfully considering the whole person and the universe of complex drivers of total health including biology, psychology, culture, economics, spirituality, and religion.

The bottom line is that what we're doing now to address mental healthcare issues is insufficient. It takes a village to care for the mental health needs of a community and its people. Desperate for answers, we've finally come to understand that we need to widen the circle of villagers who are invited to be part of the care team.

Developing a new culture and workflow that encourages communication and collaboration between those team members is our bridge to a better tomorrow.

CHAPTER 68

THE FIFTH HUMOR

Humorism was an Ancient Greek and Roman approach to medicine that attempted to explain the makeup and workings of the human body. Hippocrates and Galen described the four vital humors (or humours, from the Latin "fluid" or "liquid) as blood, phlegm, yellow bile, and black bile. Good health (or eukrasia) represented an equilibrium between the four humors and illness (dyscrasia) was due to separations of or imbalances between the humors.

Later scholars associated Empedocles' four earthly elements (earth, fire, water, and air) with the four humors and different seasons, ages, qualities, organs, and temperaments. An example of this would be the blood humor being linked with the spring season, infancy age, air element, liver organ, warm and moist quality, and sanguine temperament.

While modern medicine has made many discoveries that dwarf these early understandings of the human body and human health, "The Four Humors" own a place in history as an example of man's longstanding quest to make sense of the mysteries of the human body.

"Did you hear about the guy who ate so many Carter's Little Liver Pills
that when he died, they had to beat his liver to death with a stick?"
— joke that my dad could barely get out, he was laughing so hard

There is a fifth type of humor, the quality of being amusing or comic, whose value in medicine has outlasted all the rest. Humor and laughter have been shown to decrease levels of stress hormones, boost the immune system, lower blood pressure, and decrease pain and inflammation.

Norman Cousins, longtime editor of the *Saturday Review*, launched a second career when he publicly attributed his recovery from a debilitating connective tissue disease to megadoses of laughter and Vitamin C. Hospitalized and bedridden with severe pain, he discovered that ten minutes of belly laughter (brought on by watching reruns of *Candid Camera* and Marx Brothers movies) had an anesthetic effect that gave him two hours of pain-free sleep.

The story of his recovery, "Anatomy of An Illness (As Perceived by the Patient)," was published in the prestigious *New England Journal of Medicine* and generated widespread interest.

Later in life, he joined the faculty at the UCLA School of Medicine where he did research on the biochemistry of emotions. Along with a small group of fellow medical students, I had the privilege of meeting Mr. Cousins in person when he hosted a dinner in his home to share his beliefs about the roles of positive thinking and healthy eating in the treatment of heart disease.

In addition to being moved by his genuine goodness and deep wisdom, what I remember most about that evening was a very healthy meal (greens with no dressing) that prompted my classmate, Tim Wells, to mutter to me, "You eat this stuff to feed the good cells; but you've got to balance it with junk food to kill the bad cells."

Tim went on to enjoy a very successful career as a lung specialist.

In an article titled "Virtuous Humor in HealthCare" (American Medical Association Journal of Ethics, July 2020), Rene Proyer and Frank Rodden define what humor is and describe how physicians can leverage it to improve human health. The lighter styles of humor are the most commonly employed and appreciated: fun, good-hearted humor that lights up a room; benevolent humor (laughing with other people about the ludicrous imperfections and inconsistencies of the world); nonsense humor (exposing the ridiculous); and wit (featuring brief remarks with surprising punch lines).

On occasion, the big guns of humor (irony, satire, sarcasm, and cynicism) must be called upon to help us effectively cope with what would otherwise be unbearable pain and suffering. Said Eugene Ionesco, "To become conscious of what is horrifying and to laugh at it is to become master of that which is horrifying…The comic alone is capable of giving us strength to bear the tragedy of existence."

An uncomfortable but illuminating example of this can be found in Katie Wilson's "Gallows Humor in Medicine" article (The Hastings Center Report, 2011; 41(5):37–45.). The story involves a bank robber (in this case, the source of the humor) and an emergency room physician named "Ben": A thief escaping from a bank robbery crashed his car, and the police brought him to Ben's emergency room for a trauma evaluation on his way to jail. That includes a rectal exam, and Ben expected the prisoner to object, as many of the big tough guys he treats do. Instead, when Ben said, "I need to do a rectal exam," the prisoner looked out at the sea of cops and said, "I guess I have to get used to it."

In a similar way, one of my favorite patients named John, a salty older gentleman with multiple debilitating medical problems, always had profanity-laced jokes to share with me during our visits.

At one of our last in-person appointments before his passing, I asked him how he was doing. He took a deep breath of the supplemental oxygen that had become his 24/7 companion, and replied with a big smile, "Doc, my bucket list is getting smaller.… (this was followed by the pause commonly employed by master comedians for dramatic effect, though in John's case, he was out of breath and pausing to take in enough air to deliver the punchline)…but my f**k it list keeps growing."

CHAPTER 69

ENJOY EVERY SANDWICH

"Doesn't everything die at last, and too soon? Tell me,
what is it you plan to do, with your one wild and precious life?"

—Mary Oliver, The Summer Day

In the introduction of this book, I stated that my goal was to tell stories that will help you waste less of the precious time you have in your one brief life.

One of my role models for not wasting time was Dr. Lee Lipsenthal. Lee was a respected leader in the fields of preventive and integrative medicine and had a passion for helping patients lead more joyful lives. He also taught a physician wellness course called "Finding Balance in Medical Life" to help his colleagues cope with their multiple simultaneous conflicting imperatives. Our medical group was one of the many beneficiaries of his teaching.

In 2009, he was diagnosed with esophageal cancer, a serious malignancy with a five year survival rate hovering around 20 percent. Despite his condition, he continued to teach healthy lifestyles. He said that his imminent death gave him more credibility with his audiences. This observation about the lofty standing conferred upon those facing imminent death reminded me of the respect I had for the hospice patient whose words about the importance of relationships helped a young and naive Dr. Chuck grow into the older and more informed person I am today.

Dr. Lipsenthal said that he learned to "become OK with dying" by cultivating an appreciation for the life he already had, including his completed missions of having a great marriage and passing on the best of who he was to his children.

He also called on the wisdom of his musical hero, Warren Zevon, who while dying of mesothelioma, was asked by David Letterman what he learned in the process of dying. Zevon's reply: "I've learned to enjoy every sandwich. Enjoy the simplicity of life. Find the joy in the simplicity of life."

Dr. Lipsenthal died in 2011, but not before publishing, *Enjoy Every Sandwich: Living Each Day As If It Were Your Last.* Find some time to watch the YouTube trailer. It features Lee meditating, teaching, enjoying time with his beautiful family, and making himself a delicious sandwich filled with avocado, tomato, lettuce, and generous amounts of bacon.

"Oh death, where is thy sting? O grave, where is thy victory?"
—1 Corinthians 15:55

Let me close with one final pearl that will help you live your best life starting today. Be like Lee. Don't wait until you are given a terminal diagnosis before you begin the hard work of defining your values and living a values-congruent life. Your terminal diagnosis will come soon enough. And when it does, you will be more prepared to accept it for what it is—the inevitable and rapidly approaching capstone to your one wild and precious life.

THANKS AND ACKNOWLEDGMENTS

As I look back on my life, the dominant thought I have is one of gratitude. And because I'm a people person, I'm most grateful for the people in my life. Without them, there would be no lessons learned or pearls to write about.

I'm grateful for family. Thanks to my late parents, James and Marie, for squeezing out a fourth child (me) and for providing me with everything I needed to navigate the world, including a home filled with love and laughter, and enduring values that continue to shape how I interact with people and make decisions. Thanks to my siblings Becky, Paul, and Carol for never coming close to beating me up and always being there with exactly what I needed, when I needed it most (candy, cash, an encouraging word, a car to borrow, a place to sleep, or post-op care).

I am grateful to my late father-in-law Allen and my mother-in-law Wini for having four kids: Greg, my wife Lesli, Sheldon, and Gina. I met Lesli one summer at church camp. I was 16 and she was 14. Three years later we started dating. For over four decades, she has been my constant companion, best friend, ardent cheerleader, and most honest critic. By helping me to see life through her alternate lens, Lesli has expanded my understanding of the human condition far beyond what I have learned through any other person, book, seminar, or TedTalk. She also gave me the greatest gift of all, our children Tyler and Kelly, whom I adored as little ones, was inspired by during their teen and college years, and respect, admire, and love spending time with as adults.

Marriage and childbirth have brought many wonderful people into our two families, each one with their unique personalities, talents, and interests. Thanks to Steve, Kyle, Tiffany, Zoelle, Evan, Liane, Rio, Colby, Chris, Rachel, Luke, Traci, Trevor, Justin, Patty, Kathryn, Julia, Jim, Quinn, Posey, Auntie Val, and the late Uncle Gilbert for blessing my life with your good company, frequent celebrations, and shared vacations.

A huge shout out to our extended families (the Chucks, Jings, Fungs, and Wongs). Whenever we get together, it's a party filled with belly laughs and heart-warming hugs. Those gatherings also serve to remind us of our rich heritage and our ancestors who worked hard to provide their descendants with a better life.

I'm grateful for my past and present church families who have modeled for me how to love God and love people. From birth until I left for medical school, the First Chinese Baptist Church in San Francisco's Chinatown was my second family and spiritual home. For the past two decades, my church home has been the First Baptist Church of Davis. A special shout out to our home fellowship groups (a small group of church members who gather weekly) with whom Lesli and I have connected deeply as brothers and sisters sharing a love for Jesus, and the men's fellowship group that convenes for an annual winter retreat on the shores of Lake Tahoe.

I'm grateful for our friends, most of whom we met through our children's activities, my wife's Bunco groups, the aforementioned Fairfield poker group, our empty nesters group, UC Davis, and our volunteer fundraising work with Serotonin Surge Charities.

"The Surge" has given me a huge leg up on connecting with some of the most benevolent and generous people and companies on the planet. Heartfelt thanks to all of the planning team members, corporate sponsors, donors, restaurants, wineries, clothing boutiques, runway models, event guests, and volunteers who helped us to produce 20 golf tournaments, 13 food, wine, and fashion show extravaganzas, two 5/10K run/walks, and a virtual fundraiser called "Great Adaptations" during the COVID-19 pandemic. A special shoutout to members of our board of directors (Lesli

Chuck, Tom Nesbitt, Brad Crutchfield, Bill McGowan, Dave Cosca, and Clayton Tanaka); former board members Tony and Juli Carlile; volunteer coordinators and event planners extraordinaire Angie Burek and Tina Szura; the Silva family (Dennis, Julie, Adam and Kristin, Robert and Kate); Mike Chun; and longstanding supporters Alan Wong and Barbara Lym, Derrick Fong, Ellis and Ellis Signs (Burr & Sharon Ellis and Dale Weathers), The Niello Company (Roger Niello), Kaiser Permanente, The Permanente Medical Group, UC Davis Health (including superstar Beth Abad and the late Bob Chason), Epic, Kaneski Associates (Kelly Kaneski and the late Steve Kaneski), New York Life, author John Lescroart, Sutter Health, Sutter Medical Group, Dignity Health, Securitas, SAFE Credit Union, and the Sierra Sacramento Valley Medical Society.

I'm grateful for the many teachers and mentors I had from kindergarten through residency who poured their knowledge into me, hoping that I might one day apply it in ways that would make this world a better place. I was especially influenced by the intentional best efforts of Lorraine Palmer, Sandra Bird, and Cornelius "Con" Dempsey at AP Giannini Junior High; JoAnn Stewart, Flossie Lewis, and Peter Dahl at Lowell High School; Alexander Pines, Craig Watson, and Joseph Kloepper at Cal; Michael Lovett and Jimmy Hara at UCLA; Jeff Tanji, Tom Nesbitt, Garen Wintemute, Joe Scherger, Marion Leff, Ken Patrick, and Ed Callahan at UC Davis; and Steve Freedman, Dave Williams, Nazir Habib, Tony Cantelmi, Jack Rozance, Dennis Ostrem, Andy Klonecke, and Sharon Levine at TPMG.

I'm grateful for my classmates from junior high through residency with whom I studied, solved difficult problems, played, and laughed. Suzanne, Jack, Robert, David, Pat, Michelle, Ray, Bill, Grace, John, Alan, Nick, Dave, Bonnie, Pete…thanks for the memories!

I'm grateful for the UCLA School of Medicine, the family medicine residency at UC Davis, and The Permanente Medical Group for transforming me from a pre-medical student to a physician. The culture, operations, and people of those these organizations dovetailed well with my personality, interests, and values. Given a choice to live my life over again, I would choose all three again in a heartbeat.

I'm grateful for the colleagues and collaborators with whom I have partnered to improve the wellness of patients, healthcare professionals, and the communities we serve. Special thanks to my teammates on the following: the Kaiser Vallejo medical center; the Kaiser Fairfield and Davis medical offices; the Kaiser North Sacramento Valley adult and family medicine department, the physician health and wellness committee, and the "Beyond KP: Care for You" resilience course faculty; TPMG's board of directors, regional physician health and wellness leaders group, and physician education and development department; Permanente Medicine wellness leaders (including Richele Thornburg, Geoffrey Sewell, Kimmie Ouchi, and Peggy Latare from Hawaii and Dawn Clark and Bob Sallis from Southern California); Kaiser Permanente's division of graduate medical education; the Sierra Sacramento Valley Medical Society's Joy of Medicine advisory committee; the UC Davis School of Medicine; and the College of Medicine at California Northstate University.

Good ideas and strong teams grow much faster with executive sponsorship, and I am grateful to Jack Rozance, Craig Green, Deb Royer, Chris Palkowski, Rob Azevedo, Rich Florio, Kieran Fitzpatrick, Rich Isaacs, Pete Miles, Robbie Pearl, Margaret Lapiz, Ellie Farahabadi, Kathleen McKenna, and Richard Robinson for their generous financial support of numerous wellness-related projects and events over many years.

I am grateful for the people who introduced me to the game of golf, including Clay Tanaka and my in-laws, and those who were crazy enough to wake up early with me to enjoy numerous rounds of the morning back 9 (Clay, Dave, Kenny, Mike, Mike, and John). Golf is a beautiful metaphor for life: every shot and every hole is an opportunity to start over and do your best; swinging down on the ball makes it go up; swinging easy makes the ball go further; the lows can be inexplicable and frustrating; the highs are euphoric and fleeting; focus, intention, and practice go a long way, most of the time; and with the right mindset and expectations, even a round filled with many bad shots and missed short putts can be lots of fun.

I'm grateful for the privilege of being a physician; the opportunity to occupy a position of trust; to start and grow intimate relationships with patients and their families; to be the first person to hear a chief complaint and figure out what's wrong and how to fix it; to stand by patients as a fellow human being as they come face to face with the morbidity and mortality that await us all; to do it all needing little more than a white coat, a stethoscope, and an intention to do good.

And finally, I'm grateful for the opportunity to write this book about the pearls of knowledge and wisdom that have come my way through the practice of medicine and the living of life. While I have delivered many of these messages as a speaker, story teller, and group facilitator, writing a book without the support of visual aids and feedback from a live audience is unfamiliar territory. Thanks to Chris Jensen, Matt Niednagel, Evan Bloom, Doug Kelly, Bruce Gallaudet, Lesli Chuck, John Lescroart, Rich Isaacs, Dawn Clark, Kimmie Ouchi, Kristine Olson, Bob Emmons, and many of the people featured in this book who reviewed the stories I told about them, for their critical review of my manuscript and numerous suggestions that I used to make this book a more enjoyable read and helpful resource.

ABOUT THE AUTHOR

John Chuck was born and raised in San Francisco, California. After graduating from UC Berkeley and the UCLA School of Medicine, he served his residency in family and community medicine at the UC Davis Medical Center in Sacramento. For over three decades, he cared for multiple generations of families as a primary care physician with The Permanente Medical Group (TPMG). During that time, he also held numerous leadership roles related to wellness, including serving as the Chief of Health Promotion and the Chief of Physician Health & Wellness for Kaiser Permanente in the Sacramento/Roseville region and the Chairperson of TPMG's Regional Physician Health & Wellness Leaders Group. Upon retiring from TPMG in 2020, John transitioned into a new chapter of his life that focuses on wellness consulting for healthcare professionals, teaching medical students, caring for veterans at a local Veterans Administration clinic, and catching up on personal relationships and his golf game.

John is the Founder and CEO of Serotonin Surge Charities (a public-benefit nonprofit organization that raises money for safety net medical care), a Senior Fellow of the American Leadership Forum, and a UC Davis Foundation Trustee Emeritus. His work has been recognized with the Sidney Garfield Exceptional Contribution Award from The Permanente Medical Group (2004), the David Lawrence Community Service Award from Kaiser Permanente (for Serotonin Surge Charities, 2009), the Outstanding Alumnus Award from the UC Davis Alumni Association (2014), and the Charles J. Soderquist Award from the UC Davis Foundation (with his wife, Lesli, 2018).

Made in the USA
Monee, IL
03 September 2021